PRAISE FOR
PICTURE THIS!

"Picture This! provides a well-structured, coherent collection of photos showing classroom procedures. It is a first-rate resource for student teachers and beginning teachers who are learning to navigate the intricacies of classroom management."

— JANET SCOTT
DIRECTOR OF STUDENT TEACHING
UNIVERSITY OF TEXAS AT SAN ANTONIO

"Having supervised the mentoring process of 1500 new teachers over five years, I can emphatically state that Rick's book, Conscious Classroom Management, *was the pivotal reference work for our new teachers in building a behavioral and procedural arsenal for ensuring their personal classroom success. His new book* Picture This! *presents the core of his work—providing simple, direct, and easily applicable strategies for teaching procedures. We are indebted to Rick for his contribution and are excited to see the powerful effects* Picture This! *will have in helping teachers find satisfaction in achieving their own success."*

— BRIAN H. PEAD, PH.D.
PRINCIPAL, KAYSVILLE ELEMENTARY SCHOOL
FORMER NEW TEACHER INDUCTION COORDINATOR
DAVIS SCHOOL DISTRICT, UTAH

"Picture This! *is the equivalent of a great workshop; when it's over, teachers are inspired to implement changes right away. The visuals in the book provide clear expectations for behavior and make it easy for students to be successful. Visual aids are especially effective for language learners, who can feel overwhelmed listening to 'teacher talk.' No ELL teacher's library is complete without this book.*"

— ALISON ALCOBIA
CURRICULUM AND INSTRUCTION COORDINATOR
TRINITY INTERNATIONAL SCHOOL, BANGKOK

"*For several years now, Rick Smith's presentations have been the highlight of our countywide Beginning Teacher (BTSA) program. Both our beginning and veteran teachers tell us strategies they learned from Rick are put to use the very next day. This book is an excellent complement to* Conscious Classroom Management *and provides procedures and visual strategies that are easy to implement at every grade level. In the current high stakes testing environment, teachers are clamoring for more time. This book and accompanying online resource provide strategies, tools and approaches to maximize instructional time, affording teachers the opportunity to reconnect with students and rekindle their passion for the profession.*"

— MATT ZUCHOWICZ
DIRECTOR, SANTA BARBARA COUNTY BTSA INDUCTION PROGRAM
SANTA BARBARA COUNTY EDUCATION OFFICE, CALIFORNIA

"Grace Dearborn's book captures the essence of what any teacher seeks in professional development or recommended reading—quick, easy strategies that a teacher can use immediately to see results. I can't wait to share this book with my staff. Already a hit among my colleagues in the district for her professional development workshops, this book serves to remind educators of one of my absolute favorite 'Graceisms'—procedures precede content. Thank you, Grace, for providing educators with another outstanding educational tool designed to help kids!"

— RUTH HELLAM
DIRECTOR OF PROFESSIONAL DEVELOPMENT
ESCONDIDO UNION HIGH SCHOOL DISTRICT, CALIFORNIA

"This book is a great tool for new teachers who may be struggling with classroom management and how to establish expectations. Students respond even better to expectations when they have verbal AND visual cues to guide them. Visual cues from their teachers help students easily refocus their attention. New teachers in our school system rave about Rick Smith's keynote presentation, particularly how his examples of visuals and rubrics for classroom procedures can be used right away and throughout the school year."

— RICHARD CULP
EDUCATIONAL SPECIALIST
OFFICE OF PROFESSIONAL PRACTICE
FAIRFAX COUNTY PUBLIC SCHOOLS, FAIRFAX, VIRGINIA

Picture This!
Visuals and Rubrics to Teach Procedures, Save Your Voice,
and Love Your Students
By Rick Smith, Grace Dearborn, and Mary Lambert

Published by Conscious Teaching
21 Crest Road
Fairfax, CA 94930
Phone/Fax: 800.667.6062
Email: rick@consciousteaching.com
        grace@consciousteaching.com
        lambert242@aol.com
Website: www.consciousteaching.com

I.S.B.N. 978-0-9796355-2-6   Library of Congress card number pending

Book Design: Mary Lambert and Alexis Clark
Photography: Grace Dearborn, et. al.
Printed in Canada

PICTURE THIS!

*Visuals and Rubrics to Teach Procedures,
Save Your Voice, and Love Your Students*

**RICK SMITH
GRACE DEARBORN
MARY LAMBERT**

TABLE OF CONTENTS

FOREWORD

I T'S A PLEASURE to introduce you to Rick Smith's new work. With so many books out in this area, it's hard to find a "stand out" selection, but this is different. In *Conscious Classroom Management*, Rick states that there are three primary areas of focus in the classroom: procedure, behavior, and content. Content has gotten the bulk of the spotlight, when it comes to brain-compatible teaching and learning. But behavior and procedure are equally important. Why not, as Rick suggests, use the simple power of visuals to help with classroom management?

The strategies in this book facilitate student autonomy and a sense of control in the classroom. The students use the images to self-assess and correct. They feel more empowered and in control of their behavior in the classroom and school. In addition, the strategies tend to lower kids' affective filters: the student stress that can come from unclear procedures and raised teacher voices is virtually eliminated.

This is a breakthrough book. Using simple images, the authors are providing a link between classroom behavior and what we now know about the brain. Each page brings the reader one insight after another. So many veteran teachers, after seeing the samples, are likely to say, "Why didn't I think of that ten years ago!" I found the book to be fresh, clear and relevant. You can't get much better than that.

ERIC JENSEN
AUTHOR OF *TEACHING WITH THE BRAIN IN MIND*

ACKNOWLEDGEMENTS

FIRST AND FOREMOST, we would like to thank all the teachers who have been using our strategies successfully, and the students who so willingly adapt to visuals and rubrics to help them learn efficiently in a stress-free way. The idea for this book came from them, and was shaped by years' worth of their constructive feedback about how visuals and rubrics can help transform a classroom from one filled with conflict to one with relative ease.

Putting that feedback into book form was like writing, producing, and directing a full-length school play: only with enormous behind-the-scenes efforts could it be made to appear seamless. Especially because of the hundreds of photos from schools and teachers all around the country and internationally, this book couldn't have been created without tremendous support from scores of people.

Many teachers and students generously volunteered their time, energy, and likenesses to this project. We are deeply grateful for their help, as they made possible the depth and breadth of the sample images and videos found in the book and corresponding website. Many are credited within the book (we tried to include everyone—our apologies if we left someone out). We are especially grateful to Joy Conway, Lucia Wahl, Manuel Castro, Karen DeTore and their students at Venetia Valley K-8 School in San Rafael, CA; Anya Gurholt and her students at Skyline High School in Oakland, CA; the students at Madrone Continuation High School in San Rafael, CA; Renee Theriault with Darlene Kenny-Hayes at Clarendon Elementary in San Francisco, CA; and with Erin Zane at Bret Harte Middle School in Oakland, CA; Gary Shapiro at Harden Middle School in Salinas, CA; Trevor Knaggs and his students at Harvest Park Middle School in Pleasanton, CA; Marilyn Livingston at Southeast Elementary in Tulsa, OK; Shawn Kirkilewski-Flora and her students at Washington Elementary School in Phoenix, AZ; Steve Will at Tierra Del Sol Middle School in Lakeside, CA; Cristine Sato of Andrew Hill High School, San Jose, CA; Karen Saura at Cornell Elementary School in Albany, CA; Alison Alcobia and the students at Trinity International School in Bangkok, Thailand; and Amity Hotchkiss and Alex Allen-Hyma at Drake High School in San Anselmo, CA.

For reading and rereading, we wish to thank Martha Allen and Kristin Donnan Standard. For layout and graphic design, many thanks to Alexis Clark.

For other support, both logistical and emotional, we wish to thank Ingrid Bartolain, Robyn Lynn Thoren, Richard Paris, Collin Clark, Zoë Tellman, Paul Dearborn, and Barbara Delantoni.

"A picture is worth a thousand words."

— ORIGIN UNKNOWN

INTRODUCTION

Introduction

CONSCIOUS TEACHING—an organization focused on supporting teachers to help students—has been doing workshops for teachers in the United States and internationally for decades. Whenever we share strategies involving the use of rubrics and visuals for teaching procedures, the level of excitement in the room skyrockets. Participants can suddenly see a clear road map for teaching procedures, and simple ways to save their voices, stop confronting their students, and do what needs to be done in a fun and efficient way. Effective classroom management, once hidden from view, suddenly becomes visible and doable. We've been asked for years to put these strategies into one handy tool. Here it is!

These strategies can help struggling teachers gain competency and mastery in teaching procedures, and they also can help master teachers go to the next step—and make their classrooms hum with efficiency and positive energy.

How to use this book

What is a rubric and how does it work?

A rubric is a scoring tool that lists the criteria for evaluation—and success—and condenses them into simple words, numbers, or images. An example would be the formula used by Olympic judges to score gymnastics. They begin with a series of criteria that will determine a final numbered score for each gymnast, with a 10 being a perfect score. At every stop along the scale, in this case 1 through 10, the gymnast knows exactly what performance elements will result in a particular score. The rubric allows for clear communication.

The same approach can be used with many procedures in the classroom. By breaking down procedures into rubrics, and reinforcing them visually, we can establish a common language with our kids and help them become more successful, at the same time reducing our stress. Because students all can refer to the same rubric, and adopt a common language for performance, they can self-reflect and self-correct, thus providing the students with more autonomy, and saving everyone time and energy.

One reason visuals and rubrics are so successful is that they provide crystal-clear road maps for students, with very little room for misinterpretation. Another is that our students have grown up in an ever-increasing visual culture, with TV, the Internet, video games, and touch-screen cell phones. They're used to symbols, visual shortcuts, and interactive self-direction.

In this book, we often present rubrics with a 1-through-5 scale, but many teachers prefer a 1-through-4 or 1-through-3 scale. Others simply use an image of the ideal score, "the 10," foregoing the rubrics altogether. In whatever combination, rubrics and visuals often overlap and blend together. For some procedures, one teacher will use a single visual; another will use a rubric of progressive visuals.

> *"Students perceive rubrics as games rather than discipline, and so they are fun."*
>
> — JILL JENKINS
> 9TH GRADE LANGUAGE ARTS
> SOUTH JORDAN MIDDLE SCHOOL, UTAH

Finding the strategies you want

You can read *Picture This!* cover to cover, look for particular solutions in the table of contents or index, or randomly flip through the pages to find sample photos that may spark ideas. Once you find an idea you like, you can:

1. Photocopy the photo from the book;
2. Use the photo in the book as a model for making your own drawings or photos;
3. Download the photo from our website;
4. Ask your students to create images that are akin to what you see in the book.

Online Access to Digital Media

All the images in the book are accessible online for easy downloading. There are also several video samples.

Go to *www.consciousteaching.com/picturethis.html* and login using the password that's on the sticker on the inside of the back cover of this book. The online resources are organized with the same table of contents as the book, so you can quickly find what you're looking for.

Tips for implementing new procedures

Trying something new can be challenging. We've found that to implement a change smoothly, it helps to remember to:

- Assume the best—students, even those who appear resistant, want to learn the new procedures;
- Provide a clear road map—rubrics and visuals are among the clearest there are;
- Teach and re-teach the procedures, providing opportunities for your students to practice;
- Be committed and enthusiastic.

When you do all four, your students will be able to internalize the new strategies more quickly, as well as get excited about them. Successful implementation of these new procedures also will help you to grow in inner authority, which will then spill into every classroom situation. These concepts of "assuming the best" and "inner authority," as well as extensive details on how to teach procedures, are found in Rick's book *Conscious Classroom Management: Unlocking the Secrets of Great Teaching.*[1]

Compliance vs. Cooperation

As you look through this book, you'll find some incredibly effective strategies for getting students to follow procedures without delay or complaint. There is, however, a potential drawback to this efficiency, in that we might inadvertently forego holding students in our hearts as we encourage them to jump through the myriad procedural hoops that are part of the school experience. Let's never forget to forge positive relationships with our students.

Like all human beings, our students are full of hopes and fears, responsibilities and relationships; only some of these are related to school, the classroom, or the topic for the day. Students are often more focused on friendships and alliances in the classroom than on teacher expectations or directions. All of this is natural, and yet it can provide distractions and/or elicit misbehavior in school. Understanding and having empathy for the wider scope of life's influences allows us more easily to guide students in the right direction, without confrontation or escalation. This spirit of

1 Although this book is designed to stand on its own, you might want to refer to its predecessor, *Conscious Classroom Management: Unlocking the Secrets of Great Teaching* by Rick Smith. It is a comprehensive focus on classroom management and teaching skills, and offers help above and beyond that offered here, including strategies for troubleshooting when things don't go as planned.

compassion manifests in cooperation from the students, rather than simple rote compliance, and colors every aspect of teaching and learning.

Our job is not just to cause our students to conform to our wishes. Our job is also to remember their humanity even as we focus on content, and on the procedures and behaviors needed in the classroom to deliver that content. It is our hope that by using the strategies in this book, magic can happen. The classroom will be more efficient and more organized, and students will have more self-confidence and autonomy, allowing teachers more available time and energy to focus on the invisible but essential qualities of kindness and compassion.

Mrs. Allgood and Mrs. Meanswell

Throughout this book, we refer to Mrs. Allgood, a fictional teacher with fabulous classroom management skills. We also refer to a not-so-effective teacher named Mrs. Meanswell. She tries hard, but is struggling. Mrs. Meanswell is not necessarily a new teacher, nor is Mrs. Allgood necessarily a veteran. Teachers of all levels of experience manifest all levels of effectiveness in the classroom. Further, all of us have "Allgood moments" as well as "Meanswell moments." There is no such thing as perfection; we are constantly learning.

Also, in cases where we refer to teachers or students other than by name, teachers are referred to with the feminine gender and students with the masculine. This is done simply to help with text clarity, and is not intended to make any political or pedagogical statement. When referring to a typical student who acts out, we often use the name "Mark." This is because challenging students inevitably make a "mark" on our awareness.

The Research

Visuals for content

According to numerous studies, visuals can enhance learning by raising students' attention levels, significantly facilitating retention of information, and promoting comprehension and transfer (Katsioloudis, 2007).

Avgerinou and Ericson (1997, p. 287) write: "We, as educators, cannot afford to ignore the fact that a very high proportion of all sensory learning is visual." They suggest that visuals can help students increase competency in verbal skills, and serve as motivation in all levels of study in many subjects.

"Brain educator" Pat Wolfe concurs (2001, p. 152), stating that the eyes contain nearly 70 percent of the body's sensory receptors, and that the "visual components of memory are ... robust." Wolfe goes on to say that visuals not only aid in memory, but also serve to increase understanding.

Marzano, Pickering, and Pollack, in their seminal work *Classroom Instruction that Works* (2001, pp. 52, 99), conducted meta-analysis of significant research in the field of education, and discovered that graphic organizers help both to increase student learning and to enhance student thinking. In addition, Marzano et al. suggest that rubrics are an effective way to reinforce student learning.

David Hyerle (2000), the inventor of "thinking maps," suggests that visual graphic organizers can assist students in thinking about thinking about learning, a "meta-meta-cognitive" approach that helps students not only to learn information, but also to contextualize it in the big picture.

Autism

Visuals are used extensively with students who manifest autism spectrum disorders (ASD), particularly as daily schedule pictorials, and as markers that quickly stimulate them to modify their behaviors or actions. One example is the use of a key ring with small laminated graphics representing different actions or directions that should occur throughout the day. Rather than telling students what to do next, teachers use these graphics as illustrations.

There is clear evidence that "visual schedules" like these benefit autistic students (Bryan & Gast, 2000). Visual schedules assist with comprehension by providing an alternate channel for learning, and are easily accessible should a student need to be reminded of the day's events (Mesibov, Borwder, & Kirkland, 2002). Teaching students with autism to follow visual schedules, rather than being moved around the classroom or through activities by staff members, increases the likelihood that students will become independent of adult-delivered prompts (Garretson, Fein, & Waterhouse, 1990).

Visuals for procedures for all students

Since visuals have been shown to increase student attention, learning, thinking, and motivation, and visuals help autistic students learn classroom procedures and become more independent, it seems logical that visuals targeted toward classroom procedures would have a great benefit for all students. Indeed, in our work with teachers, we have received overwhelming anecdotal evidence suggesting that these strategies and approaches make a huge positive impact.

We invite you to do your own research. Prior to using one of the visuals or rubrics in this book, measure the relative success of what you are already doing. For example, try timing a particular transition. Then, after implementing a visual or rubric strategy, measure again, and see for yourself the clear benefits for your classroom.

Whether or not you conduct your own research, we think you'll find, as thousands of other educators have found, that the use of rubrics and visuals for classroom and schoolwide procedures is a kind and easy way to make a difference.

Finally, please feel free to contact us at Conscious Teaching to let us know what's working, and to share your new ideas for using *Picture This! Visuals and Rubrics to Teach Procedures, Save Your Voice, and Love Your Students.*

*"The eye's a better pupil
And more willing than the ear,
Fine counsel is confusing,
But example's always clear ...."*

— FROM "I'D RATHER SEE A SERMON"
BY EDGAR A. GUEST

HOW TO MAKE
PHOTO VISUALS
FOR PROCEDURES

How to Make Photo Visuals for Procedures

TEACHERS, LIKE EVERYONE, have different levels of technical know-how. This chapter is designed to meet the needs of the majority of readers. If you're familiar with using digital cameras and PowerPoint[1], and with moving files around on your computer, then our technical instructions might seem too simple. If that's the case, no problem—please skip them. If you aren't very experienced with the technology, our instructions might seem too complicated. In this case, please consult a tech-savvy colleague, or check the owner's manuals for your camera and/or computer.

Whether or not you shoot your own photos, the same procedures outlined here can be used to manipulate and process them. Remember, you don't need to use photos to make effective visuals for procedures; drawings can work just as well.

Note: Please check with your administration regarding the legality of taking and using photographs of students. This is explained in more detail at the end of this chapter.

Step 1: Getting photos onto your computer

It's easiest to use a digital camera or a smart phone with a high resolution camera. Both will come with cables (usually a USB) that will allow you to transfer ("upload") your pictures onto your computer. With a smart phone, you can also email the photos to yourself, and then save them from your email to your computer.

If you use a non-digital (traditional) camera, then you can scan your printed photos into your computer. Or, you can make large prints of the photos, and place them on the wall of your classroom.

Step 2: Working with photos that are on your computer

There are several things you can do with your photos:
- Put them into PowerPoint (Step 3A);
- Print them on your printer;
- Send them to an on-line print shop for high quality printing (Step 3B);

---

1 Note: Keynote for the Mac is very similar to PowerPoint; double-check for minor procedural differences.

- Transfer them to an external flash drive, to be brought to a print shop, such as FedEx/Kinkos (Step 3C);
- Email them to yourself, so you can access them at a print shop, without having to use an external flash drive (Step 3C);
- Transfer photos onto overhead transparencies (Step 3D).

The sections below describe these options in more detail.

Step 3A: Inserting photos into PowerPoint

Open PowerPoint and begin a new presentation. Once a blank slide appears, you can choose "INSERT" from the top drop-down menu. Then choose "PICTURE" and then "FROM FILE" (or, in Mac, just browse through your Finder). Now click on the folder where you saved your photos. If you don't remember where you saved them, try "My Pictures" (or, on Mac, the "Pictures" folder in your Finder.)

Once you have found your photos, click on the one you want, and then click on "INSERT." The photo will now appear in your PowerPoint slide. You can "drag" the photo to move it, and/or "drag" the corners of the photo to change the size.

Step 3B: Printing photos through an on-line print shop

An on-line print shop, such as www.shutterfly.com or www.ofoto.com, will allow you to make simple modifications to the photos, like cropping and red-eye reduction, and then print them in any size you want on either matte or glossy paper. The finished photos are then mailed to your home or school. This option is by far the most user-friendly and quite inexpensive, as well. Simply go to the website you want, and follow their step-by-step directions.

Step 3C: Printing photos at a print shop, such as FedEx/Kinkos

Get your photos to the print shop by using a flash drive or by emailing the photos to yourself, and then using the computer at the print shop to download your photos. Many drug stores now have printing kiosks that provide a similar service; or, sometimes you can upload directly to their websites and skip the kiosk completely.

Going to a print shop or drug store is generally more time consuming and expensive than using an online print shop. The advantage is that there are people there to help you, and you get your printed photos right away.

Step 3D: Creating overhead transparencies

There are several options:

- Print the images directly onto overhead transparencies from your computer;
- Print hard copies of the photos and photocopy them onto overheads;
- Take the hard copies to a print shop, where they can be copied onto overhead transparencies;
- Hand-draw images and pictures onto your overheads. You can use rectangles to represent desks and circles to represent students. This is by far the easiest method.

Please note: Make sure that the transparencies you put into your printer or copy machine are the right type. Melting a transparency in your printer or copier can ruin your whole day ....

Step 4: Adding graphics (optional)

Once you have printed the photos, you can add whatever graphics you want, such as numbers, arrows or titles. In PowerPoint you can add these things directly onto the slides (use the toolbar on the bottom of the screen), but with hard copies you need to create graphics separately and then paste or tape them to the photos—or just draw graphics directly on the photos.

Step 5: Display photos

- PowerPoint: Display the photos on a screen by using an LCD projector, a Smartboard, or a TV screen, using special connector cables;
- Printed photos or posters: Display them on a wall or on the board, either permanently or only as needed;
- Overheads: Keep them handy, to be used when needed.

Bright Ideas

Taking Good Photos

Close-ups of a single student or two, representing a particular behavior, usually make the best photos, but you'll want whole-class or group shots, as well. Natural lighting is best, but not necessary. You don't need a fancy camera or lenses to get good, usable photos. It's more important that you are comfortable with the camera you are using. If you're using a digital camera, take lots of photos, so you have many options from which to choose.

Alternatives to Photos of Students

If it's too much trouble or you can't get permission to photograph the kids, consider using your colleagues instead. Your students might enjoy seeing their teachers posing as less-than-model students. Also, you can skip photos altogether and use drawings, diagrams, or clip-art—and you can ask the kids to make them. One approach is to put the students in small groups and assign a different visual to each group. Your students will be especially motivated to follow procedures that they had a hand in designing.

Permanent or Temporary Images

Some images, such as how to organize a bookshelf, can be permanently posted on the bookshelf. Other images can be shown (on a screen, the board, or a poster) only when you are teaching, reinforcing, or using the particular procedure that the image represents. Setting up science labs would be an example of this. Most images and rubrics lend themselves naturally to either permanent or temporary posting. In general, post something permanently when it is an ongoing, daily procedure or classroom rule. If you are using a rubric or image to teach something that is specific to your lesson, then post it only during that lesson.

Using Our Photos

If you don't want to make your own photos, or until you have the time to make your own, you can download the photos from this book from

Bright Ideas

our website, *www.consciousteaching.com/picturethis.html*, to print and use. Our visuals will provide a twofold benefit: they'll work to clarify your procedures, and they'll motivate your students to want to create their own visuals.

Legal Issues

A. Check with your administration about legal issues regarding taking and using photos of your students. Most schools and districts allow at least limited, in-class use of photos of students. Nonetheless, prior to taking photos, make sure that your school allows this.

B. If your administration approves, send a permission slip home asking permission to take and use photos of kids as they demonstrate procedures in the classroom. Use a "right of refusal" type of permission slip such as: "If you don't want your child to participate, please notify me within one week by signing below and returning this slip or by contacting me directly." Make sure that your administration approves the permission slip that you send home. Often, your administration has standard parent permission slips that can be used either as-is or with easy modification. Please don't require students to participate in photos unless they want to, even if you have their parents' permission.

C. If you use photos from our website (*www.consciousteaching.com/picturethis.html*), you have permission to use them only in your classroom, in the spirit and manner in which they were intended.

Vision and the Brain

> *"Not only are visuals powerful retention aids, but they also serve to increase understanding."* Pat Wolfe (2001, p. 153)

Making Visuals: Quick Reference

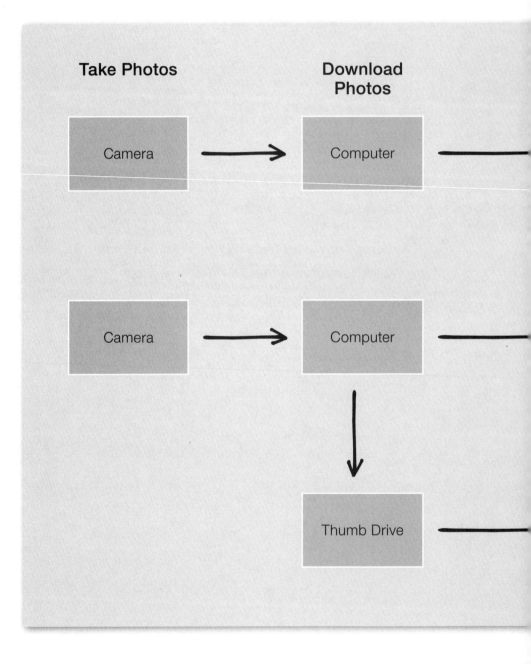

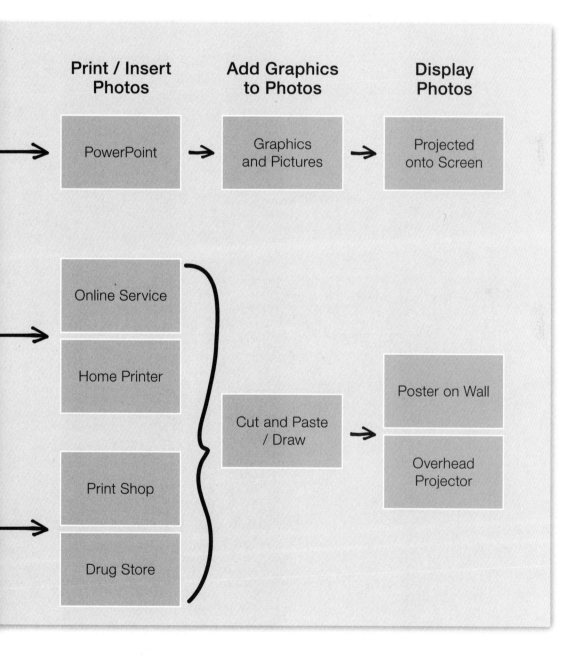

2

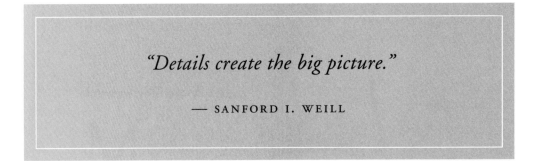

"Details create the big picture."

— SANFORD I. WEILL

STARTING A
CLASS OR LESSON

The Beginning of Class

MRS. MEANSWELL wants all her students seated, with their notebooks open and pencils ready, by the time the bell rings to start class. She tries politely asking her students to settle down and get out their belongings, but the students are slow to respond. She sometimes ends up raising her voice to the point of nagging and yelling, just to get the students ready to learn. She doesn't want to badger them, but is at a loss as to what to do.

How can we get class started on time and have our students ready with their materials, while maintaining a warm and welcoming classroom environment?

Mrs. Allgood says

Display a visual image of the surface of a student desk, with necessary materials out and ready *(see image 1 on opposite page)*.

If you require students to have their books open to a certain page, you can create a reusable visual or picture of an open textbook on an overhead (or on a poster or in PowerPoint). Then write in the page number with an erasable pen, making it possible to use the same visual each time you need to convey this information. In PowerPoint, you simply type in the new page number, and on a wall poster you stick a Post-it® note or piece of paper to the image of the open book. If used routinely, the kids will come to rely on this gentle reminder of how to get ready and focused, making one fewer thing they need to worry about upon entering the room. Both your stress and your students' stress will be reduced *(images 2A–2D)*.

Variation: If you start class with a specific activity, like sustained silent reading (SSR) or a problem of the day, use a visual to remind students of how their desks should look and what they should be doing at the beginning of class *(image 1)*.

1. Ready to Begin

Page #

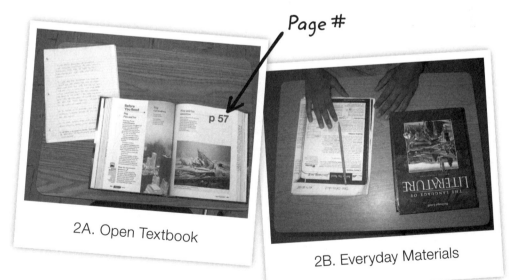

2A. Open Textbook

2B. Everyday Materials

2C. Open Textbook

2D. Everyday Materials

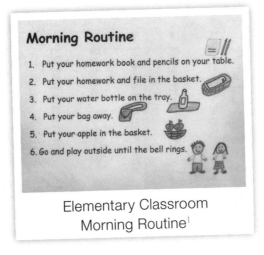

Elementary Classroom
Morning Routine[1]

"The rubrics allowed me to use consistent language and to eliminate unnecessary repetitions; I could merely refer to the rubric. My principal was so impressed with the change in my classroom that he gave me a principal's award for creating a culture of calm."

— BARBARA TRIGGS
8TH GRADE ENGLISH AND SOCIAL STUDIES
JOHN HAY ACADEMY, CHICAGO PUBLIC SCHOOLS

Headings on Papers

MRS. MEANSWELL requires her students to place a standard heading on all their papers. She uses these headings to help her label student work, so she can more easily grade it, record the grades, and pass the work back to her students. It also helps her students keep track of their assignments. However, her students often are inconsistent with their headings, and her verbal attempts to keep them on track tend to slow the class down, increase her sense of aggravation, and detract from the positive, organized, unified environment she is trying to establish.

How can we get students to consistently put the proper heading on their papers, without nagging them or repeating ourselves?

Mrs. Allgood says

1. Create a poster that illustrates the proper heading (*image 1*), and color-code each element of the heading. For example, if you want the heading to include the student name, date, and class period, then try writing the student name in black, the date in green, and the class period in orange.

2. When circulating through the classroom, if you see that Mark, for example, doesn't have the date on his paper, point to the poster and say "green" and move on. It will train Mark's brain to focus on the poster, as opposed to consistently relying on you to tell him what to do (*image 2*).

Bright Ideas

The reason for choosing a poster in this example, as opposed to PowerPoint or an overhead, is that some teachings require constant "road maps" that are always accessible, in plain view, on the wall. Creating proper headings on papers is likely to be an ongoing issue, and repeatedly stopping to flash the model on the screen simply takes too long. Some teachers use PowerPoint or an overhead initially to teach the expectation for headings on papers, and then later refer to the wall poster.

1. A Visual Poster

2. Color-coded

Materials Set-Up

MRS. MEANSWELL'S students love hands-on activities such as labs, projects, and simulations. However, the set-up of these activities can be a laborious and stressful process, where students take up unnecessary class time—not to mention Mrs. Meanswell's energy. Her students often end up missing materials, or with the wrong materials at their desks. She doesn't have the time to set things up in advance for her students, and she doesn't have the energy to play the role of "materials police," yet she knows that the hands-on activities are a great benefit for her students, both socially and academically.

How can we help our students collect what they need for an activity in an efficient and stress-free manner?

Mrs. Allgood says

Display a visual that shows exactly what items need to be on student desks or lab tables. The sample on the facing page shows a lab table with various items on it *(image 1)*. You can number each item so that when a student is missing a particular item, you can reference the number while pointing to the screen. This will help train the student's brain to focus on the visual, rather than relying on your words. In addition, you can provide a checklist handout, correlating items by their number, so students can check off each item that they put in place on their desk or lab table.

This can be used for anything that involves setting up—from science labs to art projects *(image 2)*. Eventually, students will rely less and less on studying the visual, and will immediately begin gathering what they need when the image is displayed.

"I used visual cues in the form of pictures to help students complete the beginning of class procedures within a reasonable time limit … Students who were taking 15–20 minutes are now able to do it in the time allotted …. It's such a goofy elementary way of reinforcing the procedure but it's working extremely well."

— CHRISTOPHER DEAN
6TH GRADE, SPECIAL ED. MATH, NEW YORK CITY

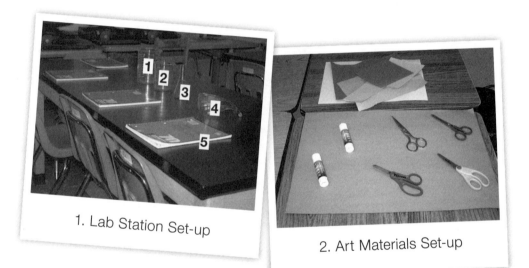

1. Lab Station Set-up

2. Art Materials Set-up

Bright Ideas

For efficiency, consider making this process more motivational for your students. Hand out the checklist to each table group of students in the class, project the visual, and then give the class a specific time limit within which all table groups must be set up, seated, and ready to go—in order to earn a class incentive.

Test Taking

W HEN MRS. MEANSWELL'S students take a quiz or a test, many might feel anxious. This reaction magnifies their tendency to lose focus on the task at hand. Thus, it's often harder to get them settled down and ready for a quiz or test than for other activities. She asks her students to clear their desks of everything except a piece of paper and a pencil, and immediately a flurry of questions ensues: "Do we need a blank paper?" and "Can we use our books?" and "What are we doing?"

How can we help all our kids get ready for testing without having to repeat ourselves, and without raising their anxiety?

Mrs. Allgood says

1. Display a visual image that shows exactly how each student's desk should look to be ready for test taking. Make use of this visual only for tests, so that students associate the image only with this activity (*images 1, 2, and 3*). If you require a special seating arrangement for test taking, then create a visual of your seating arrangement and pair it with an aerial view of a student desk.

1. Open-book Test Materials

2. Scantron Test Materials

3. Pop Quiz Materials

Seating Charts and Arrangements

MRS. MEANSWELL occasionally rearranges the seating in her classroom. Sometimes she simply changes the arrangement of the desks in the room, and sometimes she shifts desk assignments by altering her seating chart. When she makes either change, her students often feel stressed and/or overly excited, resulting in complaints, fidgeting, and disruptions.

How can we efficiently assign our students new seats and seating arrangements, in a clear and relatively stress-free way?

Mrs. Allgood says

To assign particular people to particular desks on a poster that illustrates (via photo or graphic) the whole room, you can simply write student names across their assigned desks. Reinforce the message by taping photographs that you've taken of students to their actual desks (*images 1 and 2*). Or, to use digital images, you can incorporate the photos of your students into your PowerPoint or overhead. In fact, there are several teacher grade book software programs that do just this (*images 3 and 4* show printouts from computer-generated seating charts). You drag the photos of your students into the program, and place each photo onto its proper desk. The result is an image of the classroom, with the desks in their proper places, and the student faces on the desks. This image can be projected onto a screen, printed onto a transparency, or handed out.

Another way is to print photos of your students, paste them into your seating chart, and write each student name next to his corresponding photo (this works great for substitute teachers—for more, see the section that follows). This also can be done with a wide-angle shot of your entire class, with everyone properly seated. If your camera doesn't have a wide enough angle to see the whole class in one photo, take two photos and tape them together.

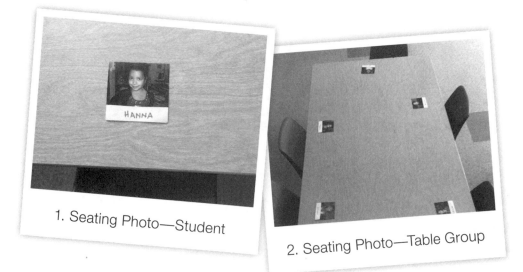

1. Seating Photo—Student

2. Seating Photo—Table Group

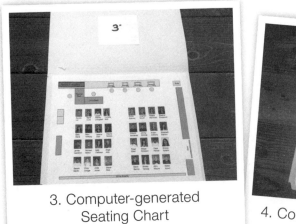

3. Computer-generated
Seating Chart

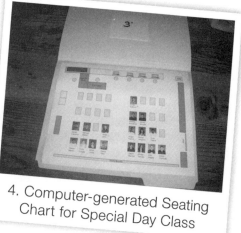

4. Computer-generated Seating
Chart for Special Day Class

Mrs. Allgood says

A simple way for you to rearrange your students, either in rows or in groups, is to use sticky notes on a folder, with each note bearing the name of a student (*images 5, 6, and 7*). This makes it easy to move around the sticky notes until you come up with combinations of students that work to keep students focused and learning together. You can easily highlight individuals from each group to be facilitators or spokespeople. In addition, you can copy your chart onto an overhead and share with your students.

Some elementary teachers initially use photos of students from the previous school year. When a student walks into the classroom on the first day of school, his photo has been pre-placed onto his desk in the room.

Display an image of an aerial view of the classroom. Looking down, students can see exactly where the desks need to be in the room. The image can be a diagram, photo, or drawing, and can be created in PowerPoint, on an overhead, or on a poster (*images 8A–8G*). Included are images for various seating arrangements.

Bright Ideas

Number different seating configurations, and post the collection on the wall (*image 9*). Periodically have students practice rearranging their desks according to the numbers. Some teachers have "seating formation competitions" between classes, as a motivator for students to practice moving desks quickly and quietly. Once students are efficient at this task, you can seamlessly rearrange formations, depending on the activity you want to do. Think your high school students won't buy into it? Check out the sample in the video section of our online library at *www.consciousteaching.com/picturethis.html*.

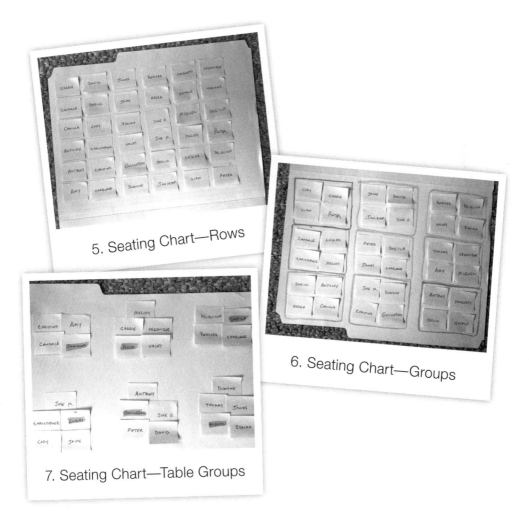

5. Seating Chart—Rows

6. Seating Chart—Groups

7. Seating Chart—Table Groups

8A. Desks in Rows

8B. Desks in Pairs

8C. Desks in Groups of Four—
Close-up

8D. Desks in Groups of Four—
Whole Room

8E. Fishbowl with Desks

8F. Fishbowl with Desks
and Chairs

8G. Desks in Horseshoe
Formation

9. Numbered Seating Arrangements

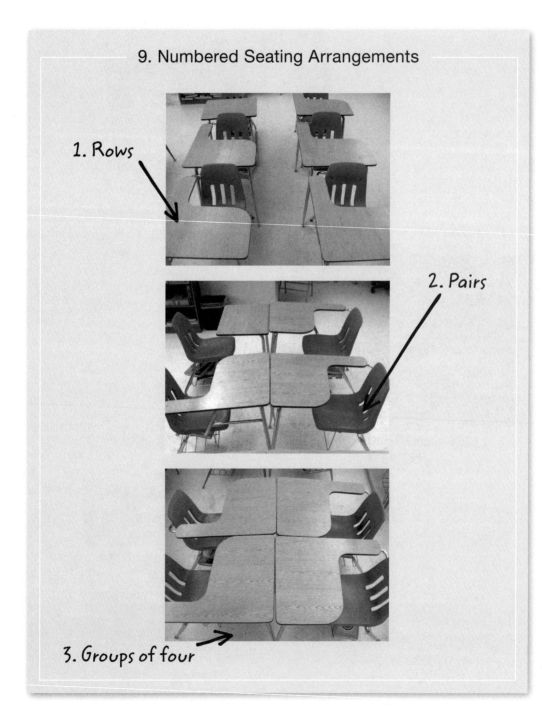

1. Rows

2. Pairs

3. Groups of four

Vision and the Brain

"The brain as a structure is capable of absorbing 36,000 visual images in every hour ... research approximates that between 80 and 90 percent of the information received by the brain is through visual means." David Hyerle (2000, p. 30)

Visuals for Substitute Teachers

WHEN MRS. MEANSWELL needs a substitute teacher, she cringes inside because she doesn't know what will happen when she's gone. Her students tend to take advantage of the sub, in part because they treat her absence as a "free day," and in part because the substitute doesn't know their names or where they're supposed to sit. This lack of structure tends to elicit the misbehavior that Mrs. Meanswell hopes won't happen.

How can we help our substitutes be more effective by knowing student names and seating assignments, and encouraging students to cooperate?

Mrs. Allgood says

Expand on the process described in the previous section, "Seating charts and arrangements," by providing substitutes with a seating chart that displays photos of kids next to their names *(image 1)*.

Bright Ideas

1. Draw attention to students as potential aides for the substitute, by using a highlighter or star.

2. Demonstrate proper ways to interact with the substitute by "catching" students "doing the right thing" in photographs *(images 2 and 3)*.

3. Have your students role play and practice proper behavior with substitute teachers. They can use the photos as guides.

1. Photo Seating Chart for Substitute Teachers

2. Substitute Behavior A

3. Substitute Behavior B

3

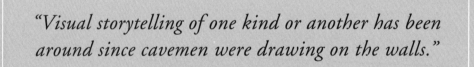

"Visual storytelling of one kind or another has been around since cavemen were drawing on the walls."

— FRANK DARABONT

FOCUSED LEARNING ENVIRONMENT

Students Paying Attention

M RS. MEANSWELL knows that social interaction among her students is an essential part of their learning and growth. Even so, she finds that her students tend to "cross the line" often, losing focus and distracting themselves and each other. She tries saying "Shush" to get the room silent, but her students either think she means that they should talk more quietly, or they ignore her altogether. She doesn't want to be a drill sergeant, but she doesn't know what else to do to keep her students focused.

How can we acknowledge students' strong desire for social interaction and still help them pay attention and stay focused during class lessons?

Mrs. Allgood says

Use a visual rubric for readiness to learn and have the students model the behaviors illustrated on the following pages. These examples communicate a message that matters to students, and entertains them in the process (*images 1–4*).

1. Elementary Readiness to Learn Rubric

2. Elementary Readiness to Learn Rubric

3. Secondary Readiness to Learn Rubric

4. Readiness to Learn

- Paper out

- Pencil in hand

- Mouths closed

- Eyes on teacher

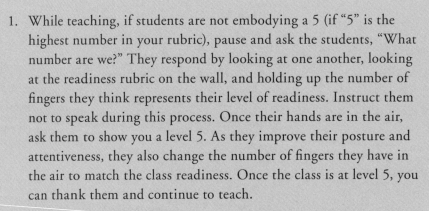

Bright Ideas

1. While teaching, if students are not embodying a 5 (if "5" is the highest number in your rubric), pause and ask the students, "What number are we?" They respond by looking at one another, looking at the readiness rubric on the wall, and holding up the number of fingers they think represents their level of readiness. Instruct them not to speak during this process. Once their hands are in the air, ask them to show you a level 5. As they improve their posture and attentiveness, they also change the number of fingers they have in the air to match the class readiness. Once the class is at level 5, you can thank them and continue to teach.

   As this process gets practiced and streamlined, you no longer will have to ask the students to show you what level they think they are. Simply teach, pause, hold up five fingers, and wait. When they have adjusted themselves into "readiness position," you can simply say "thank you," and continue teaching.

2. If you want students to sit properly on the carpet, use a visual rubric much like the ones shown *(image 5).*

5. We're Ready to Learn Rubric

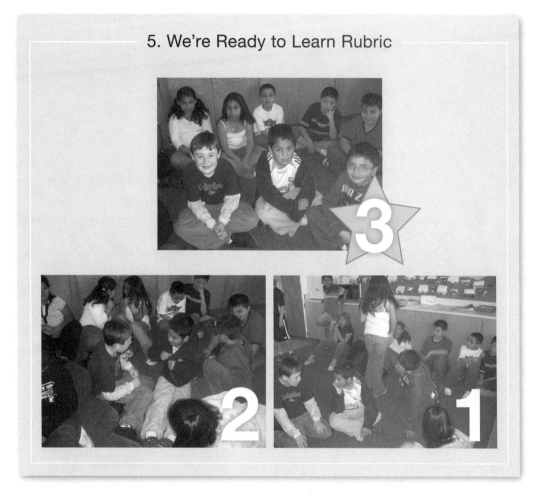

"I introduce the posters by modeling the expected behaviors for each step. If I notice the children aren't following instructions, I point to the poster and ask them to try it again. I give positive praise when students demonstrate the skill. I use these helpful posters year after year."

— MICHELLE PARR
CADRE ASSOCIATE
WESTMONT ELEMENTARY SCHOOL, NEBRASKA

Student Volume

MRS. MEANSWELL tries to foster a learning environment that is exciting and engaging for her students. In their excitement, some of her students often raise their voices to levels that disturb others. She repeatedly reminds her students to speak more softly, but it takes a lot of her focus and only works for short periods of time. Her students try to be quieter, but despite her reminders, they often forget, resulting in a loud and disruptive classroom. She sometimes feels like a "classroom volume traffic cop" who expends a lot of her energy on "flagging down" her high-volume students.

How do we help our kids self-monitor and adjust the volume of their voices without losing ours, and without stifling their excitement about learning?

Mrs. Allgood says

For individual students

Meet privately with Mark, and have him practice four different volume levels. Assign each volume level a number, from 1 to 4, so that silence is a 1, a whisper is a 2, normal talking is a 3, and loud volume is a 4. Next, discuss with him various social situations that require levels of volume that correlate to the numbers. Where would a 1 be appropriate? Where would a 3 be appropriate? Just prior to an activity in class that requires a low volume, remind Mark of the number that is appropriate.

Note: this strategy also can work great at home.

Variation: Do this same strategy for students who tend to be too quiet in class. Have them practice appropriate volume levels for oral reports, asking questions in a class discussion, and talking to the teacher one-on-one.

1. Volume Level Rubric

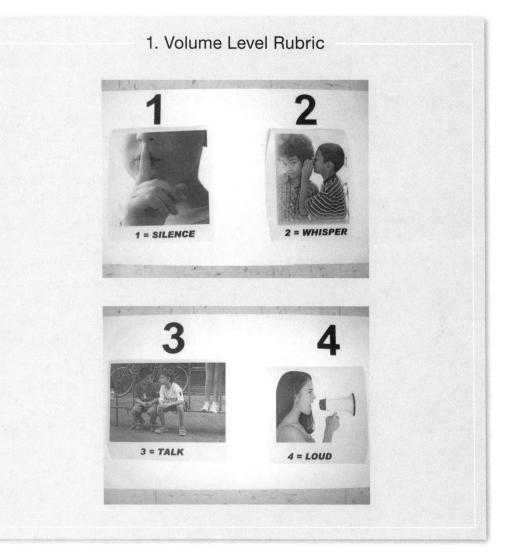

Mrs. Allgood says

For the whole class

Solution 1: Use the rubric on a class-wide level, and have everyone practice together (*image 1*). Students can then rate themselves during independent work by holding up the corresponding number of fingers. Use stop lights—green, yellow, and red—and point an arrow to the color that represents the appropriate volume (*image 2*).

Solution 2: Play soft instrumental music in the background during independent work. Let the students know that if they can't hear the music, then they are too loud. If you can't hear it, reserve the right to turn off the music and have students work silently.

Solution 3: Create a visual that represents being quiet, for example the "Shhh sign" of finger to lips (*image 3*). When students are getting too noisy, use a sound signal to get their attention and display the visual. This can be done on the overhead, on the board, by holding the visual in your hand, or by attaching it to a stick and holding up the stick as a visual instruction. If only one group is too loud, place the image on the middle of their table, or show it to each member briefly and then move away once they have adjusted their volume.

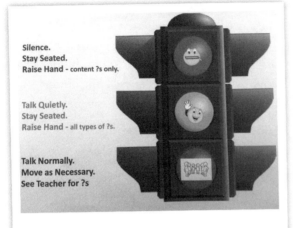

Silence.
Stay Seated.
Raise Hand - content ?s only.

Talk Quietly.
Stay Seated.
Raise Hand - all types of ?s.

Talk Normally.
Move as Necessary.
See Teacher for ?s

2. Stop Light for Volume

3. Shhh Sign

Staying on Task

Mrs. MEANSWELL does her best to keep her students on task and focused while they are doing independent work. Still, her students frequently wander off task, and often she finds herself asking her students to "sit down," "get back to work," or "stop talking." Her students feel agitated, and respond by resisting her requests. She doesn't want to yell or pester, but doesn't know how else to keep her students focused.

How can we encourage kids to stay on task during independent work, without raising our voice or getting into a public debate or battle with them?

Mrs. Allgood says

Think of the most common things you say to students while they are working independently or in pairs in their seats. For example, "Please stay in/return to your seat," "Take out a piece of paper," "Focus on the reading," "Raise your hand if you need help," "Calm down," "Stop talking," "Start writing," "Put that (cell phone, video game, food) away," as well as "Excellent work," and "Thank you." For each of these comments, take a photo or use diagrams or clip-art that represent(s) each statement, and place these in a folder, or on a ring which you can carry with you. While kids are working and you are circulating, if you see that A student could use a reminder, silently show him the corresponding photo. Once he self-corrects, continue circulating.

Variation: If Mark is having ongoing difficulty staying on task, create a small photo book just for him. After school or at lunch, do a "photo shoot" with Mark, taking photos of his demonstrations of correct behaviors. Every day when he comes into the room, place the photo book on his desk, closed. If he gets off task during class, walk to his desk and open the book to the appropriate photo that shows what he should be doing.

Bright Ideas

Make photos small enough, perhaps two inches square, to be put on a key ring. This will make it easier to carry around with you as you circulate through the class. Change the images every so often to retain the novelty.

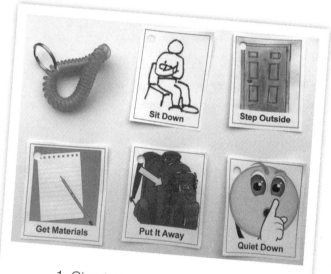

1. Circulation Ring Components

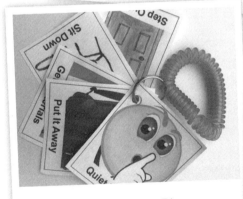

2. Circulation Ring

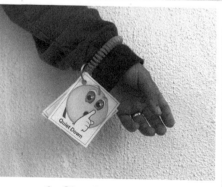

3. Circulation Ring Used by Teacher

Tattling or Complaining

MRS. MEANSWELL'S students often like to tattle or complain. If she allows it, she'll lose precious class time, while potentially encouraging her students to be mean and petty with each other. However, if she doesn't give her students a forum for airing their concerns and grievances, then they might not feel safe, she may lose a sense of class community, and most important, she may miss hearing about important matters. The whole issue is a source of frustration for her and her students, as she ends up making what seem like random decisions about when to listen to student complaints and when to ignore them.

How do we let kids feel heard when they have a complaint or concern, without taking up class instructional time?

Mrs. Allgood says

For younger students

Place a picture of an ear, a photo of the President, or a stuffed animal on the side board (*images 1A, 1B, 2, 3, and 4*). When students come to you to tattle or complain, point to the poster and tell them to "tell it to the ear (or the President or the tattle teddy)." Students will line up just for a chance to tattle to one of these inanimate objects! If you are concerned that students might be tattling about something serious, you can add a tattle book or tape recorder near the poster so that students can write or record their tattle. Then you can read or listen to these later to make sure there was nothing serious that needed your actual attention.

For older students

Have a box available for students to submit their complaints and concerns. You can require that they write during their free time, rather than class time, thus eliminating all but the most pressing concerns. You can encourage students to include notes

1A. Tattle Man

1B. End of Recess Tattling

2. Tattle Teddy

3. Tattle Ear

Mrs. Allgood says

of appreciation as well. Later, you can read what kids have said, and ascertain if there is anything critical that needs your attention or intervention.

Bright Ideas

Teach students the difference between tattling and reporting. Tattling is an attempt to get another student in trouble; reporting is an attempt to get another student out of trouble. When Mark comes to tattle, use a special hand signal (that you've previously taught to the kids) to get him to reflect to see if he is tattling or reporting. Often, once you use the hand signal, Mark will stop, think for a moment, and then return to his seat. Another way to explain this to kids is to ask them, "Is what you want to tell me hurting your body? Is it hurting your feelings? Is it hurting someone else's body or feelings?" If the answer is "no" to these questions, then the student can tell it to the ear, drop a note in the tattle box, or speak to the tape recorder.

Don't allow anonymous complaints. This reduces frivolous complaints and makes it easier for you to effectively follow up on important student concerns.

It may be beneficial to have a class community meeting, where you clarify the difference between tattling and reporting. Don't forget to also have a forum for students to publicly share their appreciations of each other—something that is often missing in student interactions.

"My students' constant tattling on each other was challenging, to say the least. I tried using a tattle poster with a picture of a man with his hand to his ear and I wrote 'tell me your secrets' underneath. Now I direct my students there and it works like a charm. Sometimes I even have to tear them away they get so excited about whispering their tattles to 'tattle man.' I was really surprised (and relieved) it worked so well."

— LUPE MORALES
3RD GRADE, MIAMI, FLORIDA

4. Tell it to the President

Students Finishing Early

MRS. MEANSWELL'S class is made up of an assortment of reluctant learners, super-achievers, and everything in between. When she provides a set amount of time for completion of in-class assignments, some of her students finish early, and assume they have earned a license to goof off. They often end up disrupting others who are still working. Mrs. Meanswell wants to make sure that all her students have enough time to finish their work, but the disruptions caused by her early finishers stymie her, and ultimately she loses everyone.

How can we keep all our students focused and on-task, even though they finish assignments at different paces?

Mrs. Allgood says

Try placing a large poster in the front of the room that says "Finished Early?" On the poster, list three or four things that students can do if they finish early (*images 1A and 1B*). These things can be generic, such as "Open your reading book and read in silence," or specific, such as "Answer questions 5 and 6B on page 131 in your textbook."

This strategy can be used in many situations, such as when there is a disruption, when you need more time to speak privately with a student (or parent or administrator), if the DVD player breaks, if students aren't prepared with their oral reports, and so on.

Variations: If you want to require students to do a particular option first, use a large cardboard arrow to point to that item on the list, or place a star or other identifying mark next to it (*image 2*). Or number the options in the order you would like them to be completed (*image 3*). Or make the first option green, and the others red. When working with students who don't read, use visuals to represent each activity on your list.

"My When You Are Finished Chart was an overwhelming success, and I look forward to using it in the weeks and years to come ....
One interesting thing that happened when I introduced it was that one student exclaimed: 'We have choices!' excitedly. I found this very interesting, because the chart was putting in explicit and pictorial form what (I thought) we already had in place in class. All year I have consistently given the same 3 choices when children finish their work early. However, all year children said to me: 'I'm done. What do I do now?' Somehow having the information on a chart with words and pictures made a WORLD of difference to the kids."

— REBECCA GONZALES
1ST GRADE TEACHER, NEW YORK CITY

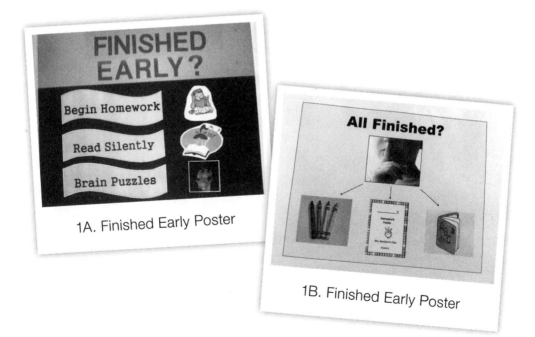

1A. Finished Early Poster

1B. Finished Early Poster

Bright Ideas

Make sure at least one item, such as "Read silently," is open-ended and can take an extended period of time to complete. It's best to write these options on separate cards and attach them to the poster rather than writing them directly on it, as you may want to change them from day to day or week to week. Finally, it can help to prepare packets, assignments, and activities in advance, so that you are ready if students finish early.

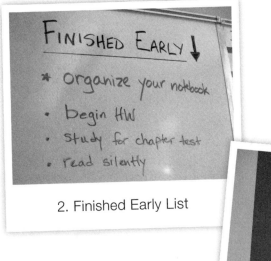

2. Finished Early List

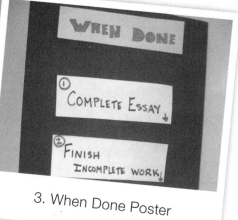

3. When Done Poster

"I have used the Finished Early poster every day since I took the course. I have personalized it to meet the needs of the scholars in my class and I must say, they gravitate to it like bees to honey. After creating the chart, I placed it on the back wall in the room in full view of everyone; that way, no one can ask the question, 'What should I do next?'

I have turn-keyed this strategy to my fellow teachers and even the principals during grade meetings, and they all commended me for implementing such a strategy. My fellow teachers on my grade have instituted this strategy as well and it is working wonderfully.

It is amazing to see students looking up at the chart after they have finished their work and becoming eager to follow the day's task without asking for assistance. This chart has helped my classroom management tenfold, my scholars are becoming more independent and responsible, and I am now able to confer with other students without being interrupted."

— DENISE GRAY
TEACHER, NEW YORK CITY

Positive Attitude

MRS. MEANSWELL knows that if her students have a positive attitude, they'll tend to focus more, feel and do better, and her class will run more smoothly. It can help when she verbally reminds her students to keep a positive attitude, but it's time consuming, and sometimes it backfires and her students respond defensively.

How can we gently and continually remind students to have a positive attitude in our classes?

Mrs. Allgood says

Permanently post photographs of students demonstrating a positive attitude, as well as a not-so-positive attitude. Students will see the photos and be reminded, and you can point to the photos when you want to remind particular students.

Bright Ideas

Talk to your students about the importance of having a positive attitude in life, as well as in class. Let them know that you will be using the photos as a way to help them succeed by being positive.

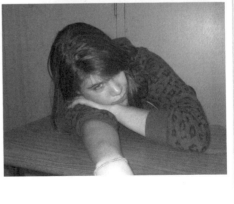

Positive Attitudes   Not-so-Positive Attitudes

Learning Students' Names

M RS. MEANSWELL knows that when she calls on her students by name, it helps establish a positive connection with them, helps with her classroom management, and helps her students feel unique and special. Unfortunately, she has a hard time learning all her students' names.

How can we learn our students' names quickly and efficiently? How can we call on them by name even before we have their names memorized?

Mrs. Allgood says

Take photos of your students, and write their names on the photos. Use these as flash cards (*images 1 and 2*) to learn the names of your students. (These flash cards are also great for substitute teachers. See Chapter 2, "Starting a Class or Lesson," for more ideas to help your substitutes.) In addition, look at yearbook or class pictures from the year before, for a head start in learning names. Use a duplicate set of flashcards, without the student names on them, to help your students learn one another's names.

Variation 1: Use your flashcards when you change seating assignments. Place student photos on the desks where you want students to sit. When they enter the room, they can easily find their new seats.

Variation 2: At the beginning of the year, seat kids alphabetically by their first names. This way when you are looking at a student in the first row you at least have a hint, because you know his name starts with an A or a B.

Bright Ideas

Schoolwide idea

Take photos of key school personnel and place the photos on your wall, along with the names of the corresponding people. You can use photos of other teachers, custodians, attendance office staff, administrators, secretaries, nurses, and librarians.

1. Flashcard Fronts

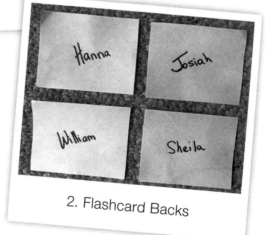

2. Flashcard Backs

Clarifying Steps in Projects

As in all classrooms, Mrs. Meanswell's students learn and complete projects at different paces. Even though she teaches step-by-step, she finds herself often repeating steps, over and over, for various groups of students. Everyone tends to rely on her as the sole source for their understanding, so she feels stretched in her ability to make a difference for all her students at the same time. She doesn't want to lose her slower students, but doesn't want to slow down her high achievers either.

How can we help our kids answer their own questions and take greater control over their own progress, without dismissing their need for support as they move through the steps of a project or assignment?

Mrs. Allgood says

Use images to document the steps. This use of visuals is content-based, rather than procedure-based, and works best in classes such as woodshop, design, cooking, and ceramics, where students are completing projects. But it is also useful in traditional classes when projects are assigned, such as the creation of a poster, timeline, comic book, or newspaper.

Example: In woodshop, teachers often require new students to create a simple product, such as a toolbox, before they can make projects of their own choosing. But since all kids work at different speeds, each student usually has to be told individually how to do each step, requiring the teacher to explain each step dozens of times. Instead, the teacher can take a photo of each stage of construction and post the photos on the wall (or simply display examples of toolboxes at each stage of construction on a table). Students then look to the photos or examples instead of going to the teacher, reducing the number of students who need the teacher's explanation in order to move forward with their project. The visuals do a better job of explaining than the teacher can. Plus, the use of visuals releases the teacher from the drudgery of repetition and frees her up to

Mrs. Allgood says

work with students in a more personal way. It also reduces the acting-out that occurs when students have to wait for the teacher's help.

In general, students succeed more when they have a model for success. If that model includes clear steps that lead to a finished project, it tends to be even more effective. This is true in many situations. For example, if you are asking students to create a newspaper from a particular date in history, they will be more likely to "get it" if you provide them with a sample newspaper (from a different date in history) that follows the required parameters; and therefore more likely to succeed. Likewise, if students are being asked to put together a lab report, they are more likely to succeed if they have a sample with the steps laid out visually.

Step 1:
Use the
Microscope

Step 2:
Use the Scale

Step 3:
Record Your
Data in Your
Lab Book

Steps in a Lab Project

"If I could tell the story in words,
I wouldn't need to lug around a camera."

— LEWIS HINE

TRANSITIONS

Dismissing Students from Class

MRS. MEANSWELL tries to teach "bell to bell," but invariably her students start putting their things away and pulling out their backpacks well before class is over. Sometimes her students even migrate to the front of the room before the bell rings, forming a large pack around the door. She understands that what's outside the door is more interesting for many of her students than the final announcements and homework reminders she wants to give, but she would love to find a way to keep her students focused throughout.

How can we maintain our students' focused attention until the end of class, and how can we dismiss them in an organized way?

Mrs. Allgood says

Take a photograph or draw a picture or diagram of what the room should look like just before students are dismissed. There are several options as to what to include in the image. One is to show students sitting at their desks with their desks cleared, their desks aligned properly, their backpacks on the floor, and all students looking at the teacher in the front of the room (*images 1, 2, and 3*). Another option would be to show just the student desks aligned properly.

Prior to the end of class, show the image (PowerPoint or overhead) on the screen. Students will immediately know that it's the "dismissal photo" and move quickly to be in place to be dismissed when the bell rings. Remember to remind the students that the teacher, not the bell, dismisses the class. If your students are not ready when the bell rings— if they aren't all seated, or if some have rushed to the door—you can simply wait until they self-correct before dismissing them.

Rubric Option: Use five images, and number them 1 through 5. A 5 would be the same as the ideal image used above. A 4 might show all students sitting, but one has his backpack on. A 3 might also include

Mrs. Allgood says

two students standing up; a 2 could show students milling about the room; and a 1 could show the students pushing against the door (*images 1, 2, and 3*). Post the five images in front of the room, above the board, and tell the class that they need to exhibit a 5 to be dismissed. When the bell rings to end class, stand in front of the class and hold up the number of fingers that corresponds to the appropriate image behind you. For example, if everyone is seated, but one or two students already have their packs on, you stand in front of the class and hold up four fingers. The students will look at your fingers, look behind you to the visual rubric, look at each other, and self correct: "Your pack! Take your pack off!" When the packs come off, you raise your fifth finger and point to the door. The students know that they are dismissed.

1. Dismissal Formation

2. Elementary Dismissal Formation Rubric

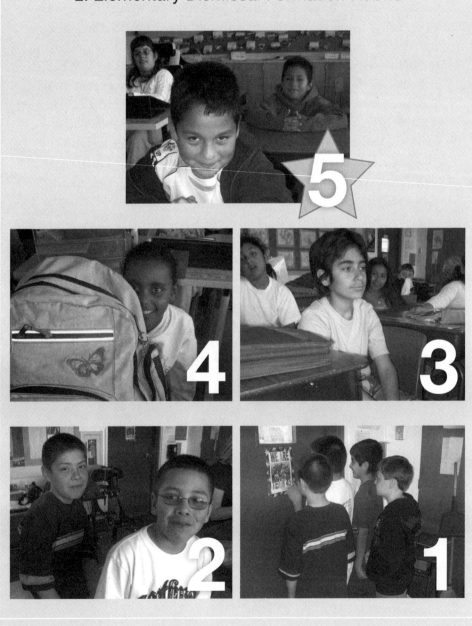

We're Ready to be Dismissed!

- Hands on desk

- Seated in chairs

- Knees under desk

- Backpacks off

- Eyes on teacher

"One technique I picked up from you that I have used VERY effectively in my high school math classes is Take 5. I have a poster at the front of my room with a guy holding a stop sign. I then listed out my 5 behaviors I need to see in order to be dismissed. I was really skeptical at first, but it really does work!

It is phenomenal. The kids police themselves. With one minute to go, they already begin saying 'Take 5!' and encourage other students to get in their seats and stop talking. I have no more herding by my classroom door and students don't just get up and begin to leave when class time is over. On occasion, I will not watch the clock and they will all look at me and clear their throats to let me know it is time to leave. Take 5 alleviates a lot of end-of-class stress because I know they aren't just going to crowd by the door at the end of class waiting to leave. They will wait for me to tell them they can go."

— LORI MCDOWELL
MATHEMATICS TEACHER, MATHEMATICS DEPARTMENT HEAD
WAUPUN AREA JUNIOR/SENIOR HIGH SCHOOL, WISCONSIN

To be dismissed from
class, everybody must
"Take 5"!
1) Hands on desks
2) Rear ends in seats
3) Knees under desks
4) Back packs off
5) Eyes on teacher/
   mouths quiet

3. Secondary Dismissal Formation Rubric

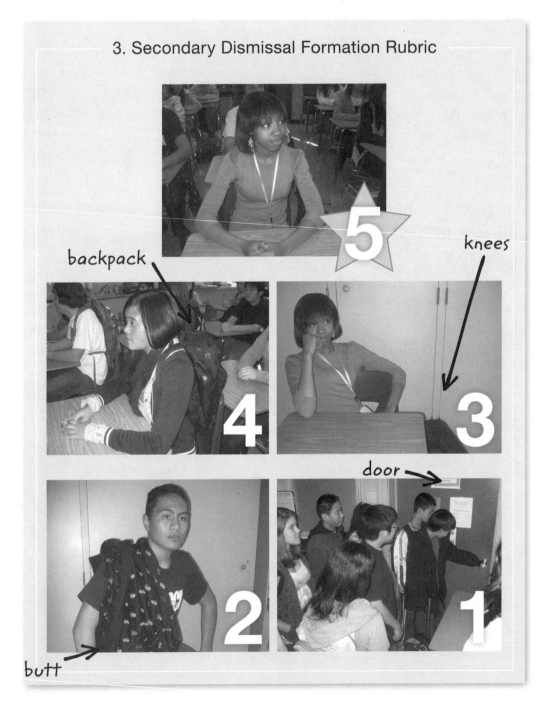

backpack

knees

5

4

3

door

butt

2

1

Vision and the Brain

"Our eyes are ... the site of 70 percent of our body's sensory receptors." Robert Sylwester (1995, p. 61)

We're Ready to be Dismissed!

- Hands on desk

- Butts in chairs

- Knees under desk

- Backpacks off

- Eyes on teacher

"After attending one of your workshops in Utah, I tried your dismissal rubric. I took pictures of my students with my digital camera and created a poster showing what behavior looked like at a '1,' a '2,' a '3,' a '4,' and a '5.' I listed the specific behavior that I expected: feet on floor, hands on desk, facing front, butts on seat, papers picked up and backpacks on floor. At the end of each period, I would hold up fingers to show the students how I evaluated their behavior. The students would remind each other what they needed to do to earn a '5.' After a few weeks, one of my students commented that we needed to add 'Smiling' to the list of behaviors because this class was so much fun. I added Smiling to the list of behaviors and the student posed for the picture to add to our rubric. Students perceive rubrics as games rather than discipline, and so they are fun."

— JILL JENKINS
SOUTH JORDAN MIDDLE SCHOOL, UTAH

Lining Up to Leave the Classroom

IN MRS. MEANSWELL'S class, the children are supposed to line up before leaving the classroom. If she doesn't exhort and cajole, the children's "lines" end up looking more like mobs at the front door. She understands that they are excited and distracted, yet she still wants them to line up before leaving.

How can we easily teach our kids to line up properly?

Mrs. Allgood says

Use a diagram, drawing, or photograph of a proper line. Place the image over the door, so students can see it clearly when they line up. Their line will improve with the visual aid.

Rubric option: Have the students form five different lines. Number them 1 through 5. A 1 would be a poor line, or a mob, and a 5 would be a perfect line, with numbers 2 through 4 illustrating lines in various stages along the continuum. At dismissal time, tell the students that they need a 5 to start walking. (Five is not a magic number. Many teachers use a 1-through-3 rubric, as shown in *images 1* and *2*).

To ensure success, take a photo of each line, number each one, and post these above your door. When it's time to line up, stand at your door and wait. As students form their line, hold up the number of fingers that corresponds to the quality of their line. They will look at your fingers, look at the images, look at one another, and self-correct, "C'mon guys— we look like a 3!" As the line corrects, the number of fingers you hold up increases, until they have a 5 line. At that point, they are ready to leave the classroom.

Bright Ideas

Have the students do the work of self-correcting and correcting one another. Choose two line leaders, rotating them every couple of weeks. The front line leader holds up fingers to tell students what the line looks like. The back line leader moves up and down the line, helping other students line up in a 5 formation. When everyone is ready, the back line leader returns to his place in the back of the line.

For more ideas on walking once the line is formed, see the section called "Hallways" in Chapter 6, "Schoolwide Procedures."

1. Lining Up Rubric Poster

2. Lining Up Rubric

"I have been using the visual rubrics for lining up and it works beautifully. Who would have thought that something so simple could make such a HUGE impact!"

— BETH ALLEN
4TH GRADE, HAWTHORN ELEMENTARY
ST. PETERS, MISSOURI

A Great Way to
Line Up in the Hall[1]

A Not-So-Great Way
to Line Up in The Hall[1]

1 Trinity International School, Bangkok, Thailand.

*"This strategy has really helped my class and the school as a whole.
We have adopted it school wide!"*

— VALERIE DOUGLAS
CORNERSTONE ACADEMY PREPARATORY SCHOOL
SAN JOSE, CALIFORNIA

Re-entering Class

WHEN MRS. MEANSWELL'S students return to her classroom from recess or lunch, they clump together in small groups, talking loudly, bouncing balls, and being generally playful—but unruly. When she opens the door, they are pouring in, often pushing at the doorway, and then it takes them several minutes to calm down and get focused. She values her students' time on the playground, but wants to find a way to refocus them before they re-enter her classroom.

How can we organize the transition from the playground to the classroom, so that students aren't disruptive in the hallways, and instead enter the classroom calm and ready to focus?

Mrs. Allgood says

Take a photo of the students lining up outside the door in an orderly way, and a photo showing a disorderly line. Post both on the outside of your classroom door, or on an easel in front of your door. Students will have a non-verbal visual reminder of your expectations, at exactly the time and place when they most need it. Alternately, you can place a photo of a perfect line on a clip-board and hold it up for them to match before you allow them into the room.

Bright Ideas

Many strategies work well in combination. For example, the correct way to line up outside the classroom can be illustrated with a rubric, and combined with a lesson on greeting the teacher at the door. In this way, students use the rubric to know how to line up, they greet you and at the door with eye contact and a hello, handshake, or high five, and enter calmly and respectfully.

If you play a "transition song" as they enter, they will know to pace their transition to be completed by the time the song ends.

We're Ready to Re-enter Class

We're Not Ready
to Re-enter Class

Images on Outside
of Classroom Door

Organizing Student Notebooks

M ARK'S NOTEBOOK is a teacher's nightmare. Assignment sheets, homework, random notes, pencils, and candy bars are all shoved in randomly. Mark often misses assignments because he can't keep track of what is due when. When he does do his homework, he often can't find it in the quagmire of his notebook and backpack. This is true not only of Mark, but of many of Mrs. Meanswell's students, regardless, it seems, of how often she reminds her students to be organized.

How can we help students organize their notebooks?

Mrs. Allgood says

It isn't enough to remind students that they need to be organized. Assume the best—that students want to be successful—and then teach organization; it is a skill that needs to be learned, step by step.

On the wall, post a permanent list of what should be in each section of student notebooks (*image 1*). Add to the list every time a new assignment is added to the notebook. Ask kids to place new assignments into their notebooks in the order listed on the wall, while also checking to see if they are missing any listed assignments. This creates a constant visual reminder of what they should have, and reminds them almost daily what should be in the notebook and in what order. Assignments can be numbered so that students can more easily see what's missing, and more easily communicate with the teacher ("I am missing assignment number 9."). Also, create a model, or a master notebook, using an extra notebook and extra materials. Have the model accessible in the classroom, and have students use it as a reference to organize their materials when necessary.

Every so often, take the time to teach and re-teach organization skills. Use the list and the model, and also circulate around the room and help those most in need.

Variation: Consider making a notebook rubric. Students can "grade" their own notebooks from 1 to 5, where a 5 matches the model.

Bright Ideas

For absent students, when papers or assignments are handed out that would go in the notebook, add extra copies to the master notebook in the inside front cover pocket. On the top of each copy, write the absent students' names and the date, or ask another student to do this for you. Teach students that when they return from being absent they should go to the master notebook to see if there are any papers with their names on top. If so, they should remove those from the notebook's front cover pocket and add them to their own. This helps students keep track of assignments, and helps you track assignment due dates for absent students.

Notebook Assignments

1. My Friend Arthur — 10-15
2. WWI in a Nutshell — 10-15
3. Technology & Innovation Qs — 10-16
4. Chapt. 9, Sec 2 Review Qs — 10-17
5. Chapt. 9, Sec 2 Notes — 10-17
6. Letters from the Trenches (x6) — 10-22
7. Trench Warfare Summary — 10-23
8. Attrition Notes — 10-23
9. Chapt 9, Sec 4 Notes + Qs — 10-24
10. Treaty of Versailles - rankings — 10-25
11. Treaty of Versailles - summary + Qs — 10-25

1. Notebook Assignments

Books on Shelves

STUDENTS IN MRS. MEANSWELL'S class put books back on her shelves in a haphazard manner, leaving her with a mess to clean up each time she invites students to use her books. She consistently asks students to put books away neatly, but they rarely do, unless she is hovering over them as they approach the bookshelf. Often she is so busy that she doesn't attend regularly to the bookshelves, and they become a semi-permanent jumble of dictionaries, textbooks, and novels.

How can we teach our students how to put books away properly, without having to micromanage them?

Mrs. Allgood says

Take a photograph of your organized bookshelf. Print a large copy of the photograph and place it next to your bookshelf. Students will be much more likely to put things away according to the photograph.

In addition, consider numbering your books with a small label on the spine. You can use letters to indicate which shelf the books go on, and numbers to indicate the order that the books go in that particular shelf.

Bright Ideas

In case students still don't align the books exactly like the photograph, assign an individual student to follow up. You can rotate this job among your students.

As with all procedures, it helps to have students practice. Every so often, make "putting books away" into a class lesson, and watch the magic happen.

This is how to organize the books

1. An Organized Bookshelf

2. An Organized Bookshelf

3. Books on Shelves

Bookshelf Yes   Bookshelf No

"Thanks so much for all the great ideas in classroom management. I don't think I will ever look at rubrics the same! After your workshop, I set up a bookshelf rubric with pictures showing three examples. Students can now see exactly how a poor to awesome bookshelf should look! It always brings a smile to my face watching my students compare the pictures to what they see. This is a great way to teach kids about cleanup without having to repeat myself over and over!"

— NATHAN GIST
GRADE 3 TEACHER, WELLS INTERNATIONAL SCHOOL
BANGKOK, THAILAND

Putting Supplies Away

JUST AS WITH THE BOOKS and the bookshelves, Mrs. Meanswell's students seem to have a hard time neatly and efficiently putting away lab materials, art materials, P.E. equipment, and other supplies. Whenever she has a project planned, Mrs. Meanswell winces inside, figuring that she'll have to endure the chaos that invariably ensues at clean-up time.

How can we gently but consistently focus our kids' attention on properly putting supplies away?

Mrs. Allgood says

Take a photograph of the supplies as you want them to appear once they are put away (*images 1, 2, and 3*). Post the photograph next to where the supplies belong. In addition, you can put the photos in PowerPoint or on an overhead, and display the images on your screen when it's time to put things away. When the image appears, students will know immediately that it's time to put things away (you can also use a special sound signal or song that indicates the same thing). They'll also be able to use the images to help them organize the supplies.

Variation 1: Consider labeling each item with a number or letter, and putting corresponding labels on the shelves or trays where they belong.

Variation 2: For certain items, it helps to draw outlines or stencils of the objects in or on their storage locations. For example, many woodshop teachers require tools to be put on wall hooks. They can use a marker to draw on the wall an outline of the hammers, clamps, levels, and other tools, so that students know to match the shape of the tool with the outline. Just before dismissal, the teacher can look at the wall of tools, and immediately see if any tools are missing.

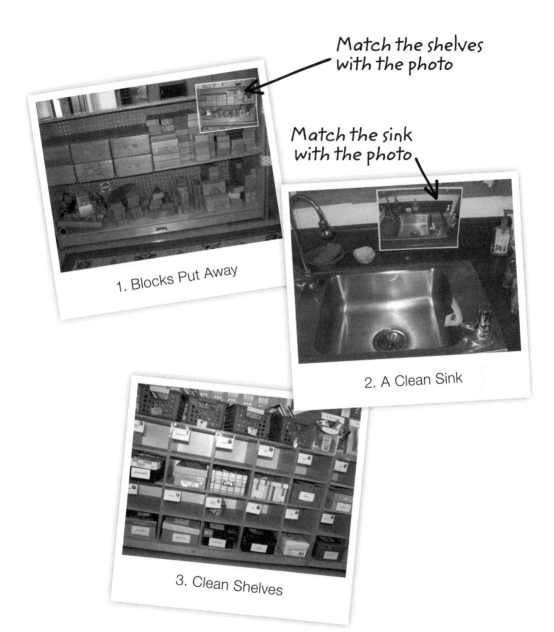

Match the shelves
with the photo

Match the sink
with the photo

1. Blocks Put Away

2. A Clean Sink

3. Clean Shelves

Cleaning Up

STUDENTS IN MRS. MEANSWELL'S class not only have a hard time putting books and supplies away, but also tend to leave messes in the areas around their desks. They often have a different definition of "clean" than Mrs. Meanswell does; perhaps they don't always see what needs to be done, and/or hope that someone else will take care of the mess.

How can we help students be clear about what we mean by "clean," and how can we encourage them to take responsibility for not only their own messes, but the general cleanliness of the classroom?

Mrs. Allgood says

Take photos of clean areas, and display the photos on PowerPoint or an overhead when it's time for students to clean up (*images 1, 2, and 3*). You can also post images of clean tables, centers, cubbies and the like on your wall.

Variation: Take photos of a messy floor and a clean floor, and display both or post both on a poster, so that students know exactly what is acceptable and what isn't.

Bright Ideas

Students often claim that the mess on the floor "isn't mine!" Let your class know that each student is responsible for the entire room. This can double as a lesson in civic responsibility. In addition, you can assign specific areas for each student or group of students. For example, when students are in rows, each student can be responsible for the area underneath his seat and directly to the left of his desk.

Have your students practice the cleaning-up procedure in the middle of the class, so they understand what to do and exactly what's expected. This practice, done when students are not frantically worried about leaving on time, will help them be more focused and efficient when you have them do it "live" at the end of class in the future.

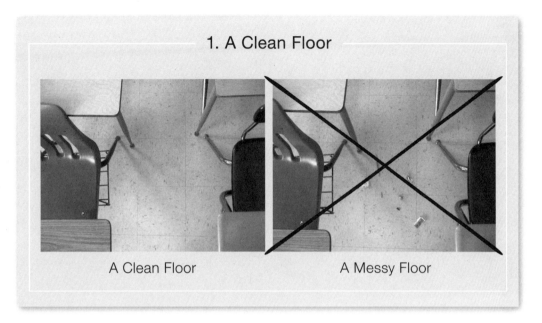

1. A Clean Floor

A Clean Floor

A Messy Floor

"This is my 7th year teaching, and visuals for cleaning up are some of the most effective things I've used."

— LESLIE CREATH
MATH/SCIENCE ACADEMIC COACH, KAUFFMAN SCHOLARS, INC.
KANSAS CITY, MISSOURI

2. A Clean Table

3. A Clean Center

"*Almost all quality improvement comes via simplification of design ... processes, and procedures.*"

— TOM PETERS

CLASSROOM RULES

Classroom Rules

A LTHOUGH MRS. MEANSWELL keeps a clear list of classroom rules, she finds herself constantly having to repeat them to her students, and often gets engaged in arguments about what the rules are and why they are necessary. She tries to assume the best about her students, reminding herself that they want and need the rules in order to have safety and structure for success, but the constant testing by her students sometimes leaves her exhausted and questioning her own positive assumptions[1].

How can we reinforce classroom rules without having constantly to defend them, and without getting into public debates with our students?

Mrs. Allgood says

Take photos of students while they are both breaking the rules and following the rules. Use those photos (or drawings, or clip-art), with their corresponding labels or explanations, as constant visual reminders of the classroom rules. Post these photos on a wall in the room for reference. You can silently refer students to the photos. Invariably, your students will end up referring one another to the photos, taking you out of the loop.

Many examples follow, along with explanations, when necessary.

---

1 For more about "assuming the best," please see Chapter 2 in *Conscious Classroom Management* by Rick Smith.

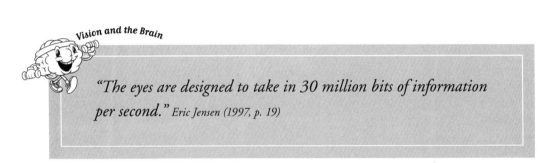

Vision and the Brain

"The eyes are designed to take in 30 million bits of information per second." Eric Jensen (1997, p. 19)

Tardiness

MRS. MEANSWELL has what she thinks is a clear tardy policy, yet her students often argue with her that they weren't late because they were "in the room" or "near the door" or "didn't know what the policy was" or were there on time but then "had to go out for a second." Mrs. Meanswell finds herself arguing in front of her class with her late students, thus siphoning off instructional time and depleting the creative energy available for teaching and learning. Part of the cause of the arguing is that even though she thinks her policy is clear, it is actually open to the wiggle room of interpretation. Her students aren't necessarily wrong for disagreeing; they're just unclear—and, at times, opportunistic.

How can we reinforce our classroom tardy policy so that all kids are clear on the expectation and have the greatest chance of following it successfully?

Mrs. Allgood says

Use two visuals. One shows a student at his desk when the bell rings, along with the caption "on time." The other shows a student who is tardy, but just barely. If your tardy policy is that students need to be across the threshold of the door when the bell finishes ringing, then your second visual should show a student halfway across the threshold, along with a caption that says "tardy." If your policy is that students need to be seated at their desks when the bells finishes ringing, then your second visual should show a student who is almost seated, along with the caption "tardy." Put these visuals on a poster on your wall as a constant visual reminder of the parameters of "on time" and "tardy." Teach the students in the beginning of the year what the policy is, and use the visuals to reinforce that teaching throughout the year.

Elementary:
This student IS tardy for class

Elementary:
This student IS NOT tardy for class

Secondary:
This student IS tardy for class

Secondary:
This student IS NOT tardy for class

Be Seated When the
Second Bell Rings

Hats

No Hats in Class

Images courtesy of Trevor Knaggs and his students, Harvest Park Middle School, Pleasanton, California.

Cell Phones / Electronics

Secondary

Secondary

Elementary

Elementary

No Cell Phones in Class

Food

Secondary[1]

Secondary

Secondary[1]

No Food in Class Please

1 Image courtesy of Trevor Knaggs and his students, Harvest Park Middle School, Pleasanton, California.

Talking

See also Chapter 3, "Focused Learning Environment."

Elementary

Secondary[1]

Secondary

Secondary

No Talking While the Teacher is Talking

Wall of Readiness

Mrs. Allgood says

Make a place on a wall in your room to permanently post the images that pertain to the rules. You can also include images of procedures that students need to see on a regular basis, such as headings on papers, or having a positive attitude. Many teachers call this collection of images the class "Wall of Readiness." It can be a positive way to easily remind the students what they need to know in order to be successful in your class.

"My Wall of Readiness has really helped reinforce the rules and routines in my math classes. I used my worst offenders as the models for some of the photos, and everybody got a kick out of that. Now I just point to the wall when I need to remind a student about something, because there is no arguing with a photo."

— MARCO HERNANDEZ
HIGH SCHOOL MATH, CHICAGO, ILLINOIS

"*Seeing is believing.*"

— ORIGIN UNKNOWN

SCHOOLWIDE
PROCEDURES

Dress Code

THERE'S A DRESS CODE at Mrs. Meanswell's school. Her students push their fashion choices to the edge (if not over the edge) of acceptability, as they try to fit in with their friends and feel good about how they look. When Mrs. Meanswell does try to enforce the dress code, the students often meet her feedback with resistance and complaints; students often argue, "I didn't know," or "I'm not breaking the rules."

How can we clarify and reinforce a school dress code without getting into verbal confrontations with our students?

Mrs. Allgood says

Work with the administration to make a rubric of photos or drawings of students dressed appropriately and inappropriately (consider the option of making them anonymous). Post these in classrooms and around the school. If a student is dressed inappropriately, a teacher can point to the posted image and point to the student, and that information will suffice to make the communication clear.

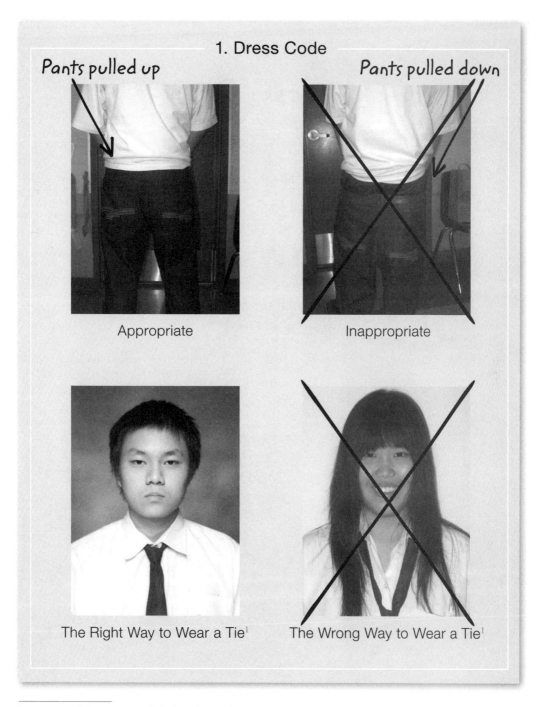

Images courtesy of Trinity International School, Bangkok, Thailand.

Uniform Code

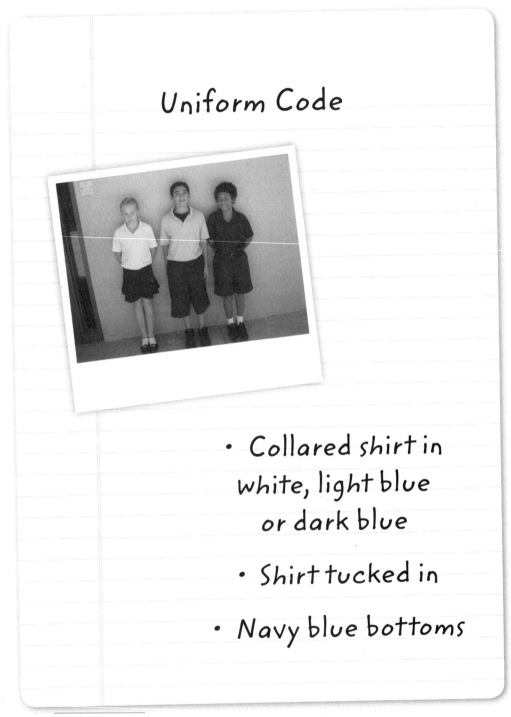

- Collared shirt in white, light blue or dark blue

- Shirt tucked in

- Navy blue bottoms

Image courtesy of Shawn Kirkilewski-Flora, 5th grade, Washington Elementary, Phoenix, Arizona.

Vision and the Brain

"When it comes to memory, researchers have known for more than 100 years that pictures and text follow very different rules. Put simply, the more visual the input becomes, the more likely it is to be recognized—and recalled. The phenomenon is so pervasive, it has been given its own name: the pictorial superiority effect, or PSE." Dr. John Medina (2008, p. 233)

Cafeteria Cleanliness

O NE AREA WHERE STUDENTS tend to shirk responsibility is in keeping the cafeteria clean. The mess and chaos in the cafeteria tend to result from a combination of the relative lack of structure during lunch and break, the excess energy that students feel when not in the classroom (or after eating copious amounts of sugar), and the more lax level of supervision in this area. When she's on lunchroom duty, Mrs. Meanswell finds herself raising her voice and entering into loud debates when trying to get her students to clean up after themselves at lunch.

How can we teach our kids to clean up thoroughly after they eat without escalating tension or making it feel like a punishment?

Mrs. Allgood says

Use an image of a clean table, and post it on the wall. When students argue that their table is clean, simply point to the poster on the wall.

Rubric option: Make five visuals and number them 1 through 5 (or 1 through 3, as in the sample on the right), making 5 an acceptably clean table, 1 a disaster, and filling in numbers 2 through 4 appropriately. Post all five on the wall. You might also secure a laminated image of a 5 in the center of each table.

Variation: Cafeteria workers or teachers can walk around the tables and let the students know the quality of the cleanliness of their tables by simply holding up the number of fingers that corresponds to the level of cleanliness of the student tables. Or, they can hold up cards that have numbers on them. Or, they can hold up cards that have the actual images on them, along with the corresponding numbers. This works particularly well when the students must be formally dismissed from the cafeteria to go outside. Instead of arguing with them when they claim their table is clean, simply use the rubric number (fingers or card) to let them know. If they are eager to enjoy free time, they will tend to clean their table quickly and without argument.

Cleaning Up Cafeteria Tables Rubric

Cleaning Up the Cafeteria Tables

Mrs. Allgood says

Other Cafeteria Behaviors

At Washington Elementary in Phoenix, Arizona, students model appropriate lunchtime procedures, including walking to the cafeteria and getting food (*images 1–8*). These images can be used in classroom PowerPoint presentations to review the procedures, and/or posted on the walls of the cafeteria as reminders.

In a second elementary school, cafeteria workers hold up cards—1 through 5—to rate or score kid behaviors, including how they enter, how well they clean up, and how they line up for their food. As the card is held up, the students have immediate feedback, and an incentive, as they can't proceed toward the line to dismissal unless they get a 5. Because cafeterias are usually quite loud, any verbal instructions have to be even louder than the student noise, which often results in escalating tension and lack of clarity. These non-verbal strategies help minimize tensions and conflicts between the cafeteria supervisors and the students. Plus, cafeteria workers get to feel like Olympic judges!

Lunch Procedures

5

6

7

8

Lunch Procedures

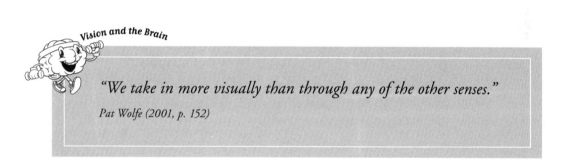

Vision and the Brain

"We take in more visually than through any of the other senses."

Pat Wolfe (2001, p. 152)

Bathroom Cleanliness

SOMETIMES THE STUDENTS at Mrs. Meanswell's school leave the bathrooms a mess. She can't be everywhere at once to supervise, yet she is committed to teaching her students to be responsible.

How do we reinforce to the need to keep bathrooms neat and clean when we can't necessarily be in the bathrooms when the kids are making the messes?

Mrs. Allgood says

Post images on the bathroom walls that show what a clean bathroom looks like. Various images can be used in various locations. For example, on the outside of the bathroom door, post a photo of a clean bathroom. Inside the bathroom, a photo of a clean, dry sink area can be posted above the sinks. On the inside of each toilet stall door, placing a photo of a clean, dry toilet can remind students of their responsibilities. Near the trash cans, place a photo of a can with no paper towels on the floor around it. While there is no guarantee that this will ensure that the bathrooms are clean, it will help communicate a reminder of clear expectations to the students.

A Clean Bathroom

Hallways

KIDS AT MRS. MEANSWELL's school are often so excited to be out of class and free to do as they please—whether during passing periods, at recess, at lunch, or while on an errand for the teacher—that they forget how to behave appropriately. They run in the hallways, block the hallways, and walk on both sides of the hallways so that they bump into each other.

How can we encourage politeness and awareness of selves and others while kids are in the hallways?

Mrs. Allgood says

Use diagrams, drawings, and/or photos to show what the hall should look like between classes. Post the images in the halls. Have teachers use the images in their classrooms to teach their students appropriate hallway behavior.

Variation: Make a video of students behaving properly in the hallway. Show it to students during classtime.

Bright Ideas

When kids need to walk with their teacher through hallways, have a photo example of correct hallway behavior on a clipboard or adhered to a stick or ruler. When kids get too noisy or display other inappropriate behaviors, stop and hold up the photo. Wait for kids to match the photo before continuing to walk through halls (*images 1A, 1B, 2A, 2B, 3A, and 3B*).

1A. Walk Quietly

1B. Walking Quietly

2A. Walk in a Straight Line

2B. Walking in a Straight Line

3A. Keep Your Hands to Yourself

3B. Keep Your Hands to Yourself

Office Waiting Room

WHEN STUDENTS AT MRS. MEANSWELL'S school are sent to the office, they often feel stressed, worried, angry, frightened, impatient, and/or otherwise uncomfortable. They tend to act out while waiting to meet with an administrator or counselor. Their behaviors include inappropriate discussion, yelling, pacing, using cell phones, or distracting support staff.

How can we help kids understand what we expect of them while they are waiting to see someone in the main office, without adding to their anxiety or our workload?

Mrs. Allgood says

On the wall in the waiting room, post photos of how not to behave (standing, shouting, using cell phone) with a circle and line through them. Next to those images, post photos of how to behave appropriately (seated and silently waiting or reading).

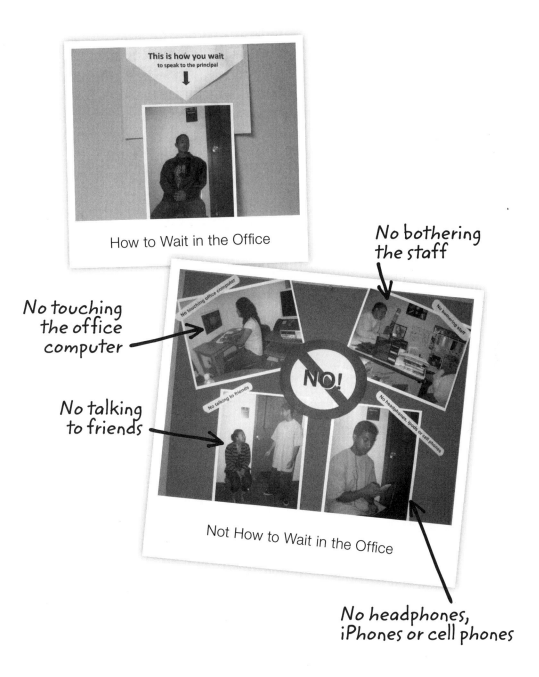

How to Wait in the Office

No bothering the staff

No touching the office computer

No talking to friends

Not How to Wait in the Office

No headphones, iPhones or cell phones

Organizing Rooms After Special Events and Staff Meetings

WHENEVER THERE ARE SPECIAL MEETINGS at Mrs. Meanswell's school—staff development workshops for teachers, or multiple-class gatherings for students—the room is often a mess after the meeting is over. Mrs. Meanswell makes announcements asking participants (teachers or students, depending on the meeting) to put things back, but invariably, she has to spend time afterward replacing the desks, tables, and chairs to their original positions.

How can we easily get participants in meetings to put furniture back where it belongs?

Mrs. Allgood says

Take a photograph of the room before participants enter. Just before the meeting or assembly is finished, project the image of the photograph on the wall, and ask participants to move the furniture around to match the photo.

1. Staff Meeting Table

2. Staff Meeting Room

3. Library Tables and Chairs

4. Library Staff Meeting

Using Schoolwide Television Monitors

M RS. MEANSWELL'S SCHOOL has television monitors in all the rooms and the hallways, for communications from the office. She knows that students love the medium of TV, and she'd like her school to maximize the use of the televisions, but isn't sure what to suggest.

How can schools take advantage of television monitors to help students learn procedures and behavior?

Mrs. Allgood says

1. The principal can walk around with a camera around her neck, taking photos of students "caught doing well" in classrooms and elsewhere throughout the school. Between classes, she can show the photos on the television monitors, inspiring students to do well so they can also get "caught" on camera. The principal will become the most popular person in the school, as students hover around her camera.

2. Emulate Harden Middle School in Salinas, California. Gary Shapiro teaches a video class there in which the students produce "video announcements" that are aired most days on the television monitors in all the classrooms. The subject matter often includes a review of one or more school rules or policies. Students in the class learn acting, directing, screenwriting, cinematography, and editing, and students throughout the school view the announcements (along with the rules!) in an engaging medium. You can view samples at *www.consciousteaching.com/picturethis.html.*

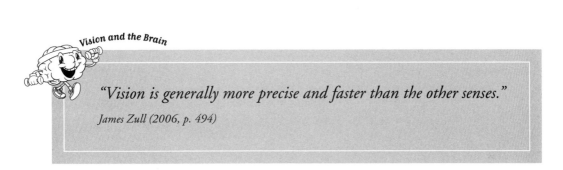

Vision and the Brain

"Vision is generally more precise and faster than the other senses."

James Zull (2006, p. 494)

Video for Schoolwide Procedures

MRS. MEANSWELL'S SCHOOL has a video camera. She would love to use it to help students learn the school rules and procedures, and isn't sure—outside of a video class—how it can be used.

How can video be used to help teach students the schoolwide rules and procedures?

Mrs. Allgood says

Emulate Southeast Elementary of Jenks Public Schools in Tulsa, Oklahoma, which invited thirty students to come to school a week before school started in August to "make a movie." Teachers videotaped students modeling proper schoolwide procedures, including getting on and off the bus, riding the bus, walking down the halls, and behaving in the cafeteria. The principal, Marilyn Livingston, Ph.D., narrated the nine-minute DVD; each teacher played a copy of the DVD during the first week of school as a teaching tool. Later, if a student hadn't followed one of the schoolwide procedures, he carried home a note to his parents, along with a copy of the DVD. Parents could then watch alongside their child, reinforcing the proper procedures. Videos like this can be made available at back-to-school night, too. In the Oklahoma school, several parents even expressed interest in keeping copies of the DVD—to use as a model for making employee-training DVDs at their businesses!

*To view the videos described in this section, as well as numerous other school and classroom videos, please go to our website, **www.consciousteaching.com/picturethis.html** and use the password on the sticker on the inside of the back cover of this book.*

"If you want to reach younger people at an earlier age ... you need to know how ideas ... are expressed visually."

— MARTIN SCORCESE

PROCEDURES
AT HOME

Procedures at Home

MANY TEACHERS at our workshops have commented that visuals and rubrics would work great with their children (and their spouses!). We've put together a few samples to spark possibilities for you to try at home.

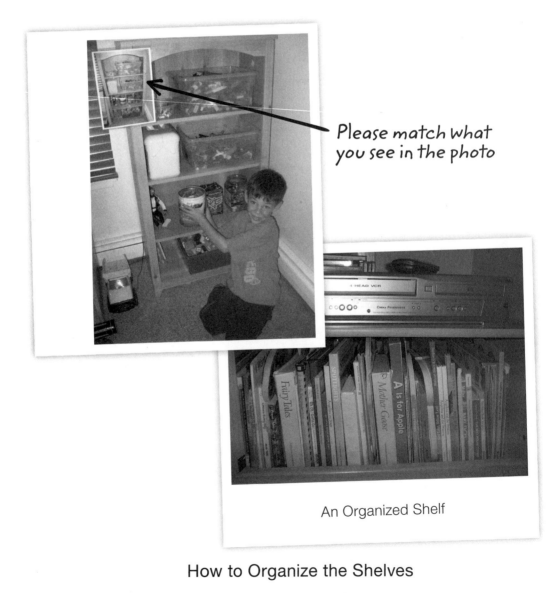

Please match what you see in the photo

An Organized Shelf

How to Organize the Shelves

Please match what
you see in the photo

How to Make the Bed

Please match what
you see in the photo

Put the Seat Cover Down, Please!

Where the Sponge Lives

The Dirty Kitchen Sink

The Clean Kitchen Sink

A Clean Desk

Please match what
you see in the photo

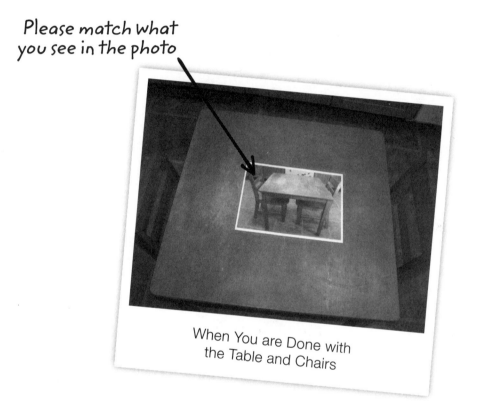

When You are Done with
the Table and Chairs

How to Stack the DVDs

How Not to Stack the DVDs

How to Hang the Coats

How Not to Hang the Coats

"*When words become unclear,
I shall focus with photographs* ..."

— ANSEL ADAMS

CASE STUDIES

Case Study: Arizona

OVER THE YEARS, we have found that very few teachers who try visuals and rubrics, stop at just one. Once teachers see the immediate positive effects of one idea, they quickly find more applications. This chapter presents two series of examples—one is from a teacher in Arizona, and the other is from an international school in Bangkok, Thailand. We kept the images and captions largely unedited, so that you can get a taste of a range of possibilities—for both the classroom and school wide.

This case study is from Shawn Kirkilewski-Flora, who teaches 5th grade at Washington Elementary in Phoenix, Arizona.

Morning Procedures:

Proof Reading

**Desk set-up on
Mon, Tues, & Thurs**

**Desk set-up on
Wed & Fri**

Morning Procedures:

Breakfast Procedures

Helper picks a partner to take breakfast outside.

Boy line leader takes breakfast garbage outside.

Girl line leader puts garbage bag in garbage can.

Uniform Code

- Collared shirt in white, light blue, or dark blue

- Shirt tucked in

- Navy blue bottoms

Listening to the Teacher

Waiting for the Teacher

Taking Notes:

1. Take out your paper.

2. Take notes.

3. If you finish taking notes sit in polite position.

Whiteboard Materials:

1. Dictionary
2. Whiteboard
3. Marker
4. Fabric

Polite position
-hands crossed
-eyes on speaker

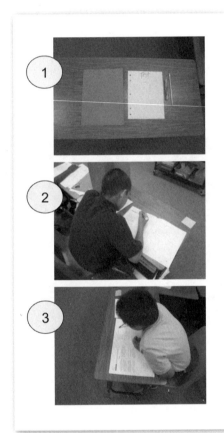

Test Taking Procedures:

1. Four Materials Ready:
   –Blue barrier & Test
   –Pencil & Highlighter

2. Highlight Answers

3. Go Back,
   Check Answers,
   Write Correct Answers

Cooperative Group Rules

1. Take turns talking quietly.

2. Listen & praise each other's ideas.

3. Help each other.

4. Stay together until given the next expectation.

5. Talk about what went well.

6. Talk about what you can do to improve next time.

Line Procedures
(Going to Lunch)

Lunch Procedure

Line Procedures:

Line Procedures
(inside the classroom)

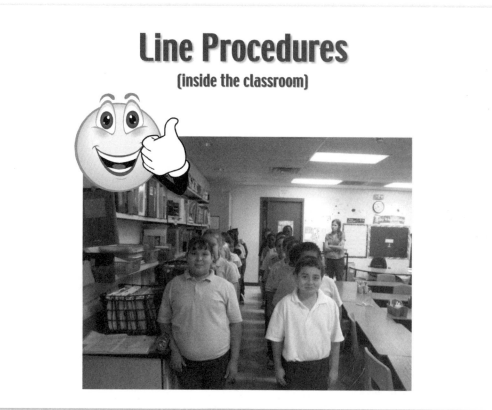

Jobs

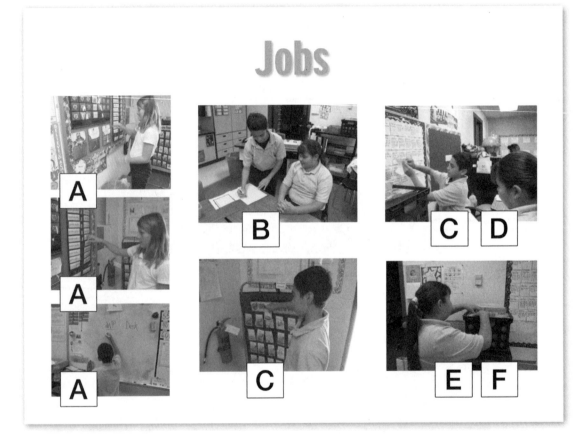

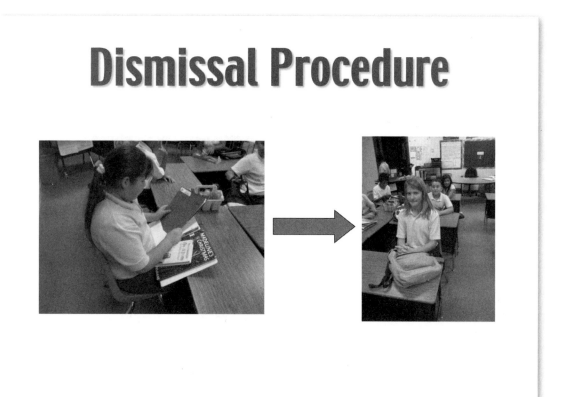

Case Study: Bangkok, Thailand

This case study is from Trinity International School in Bangkok, Thailand. Photos are provided by Alison Alcobia, the Curriculum and Instruction Coordinator.

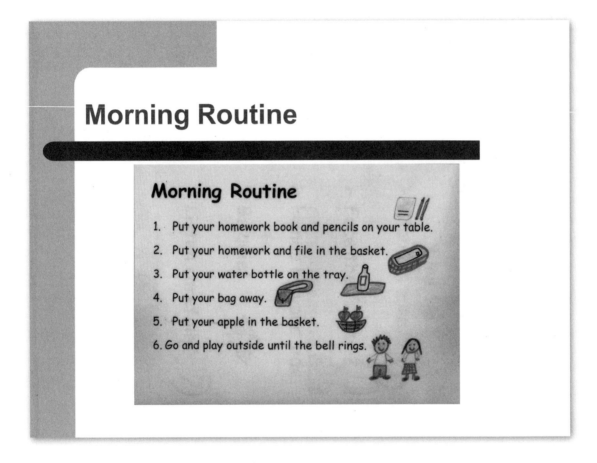

Line up

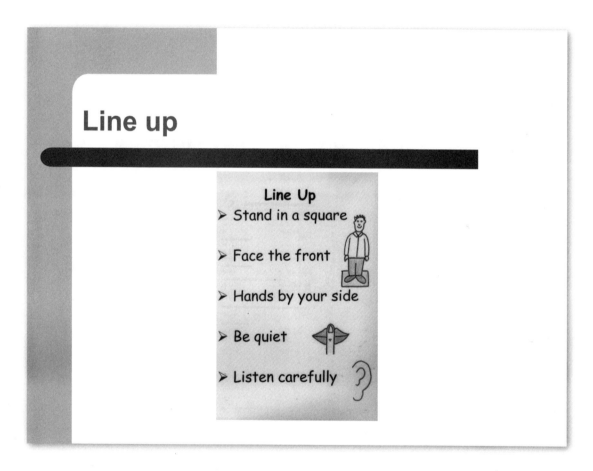

Lining Up

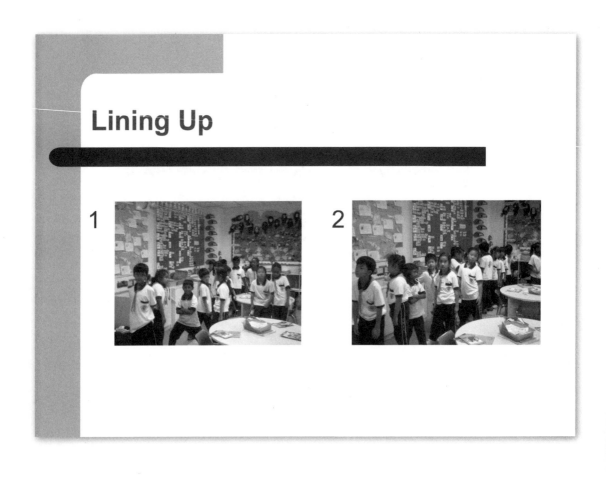

Lining Up

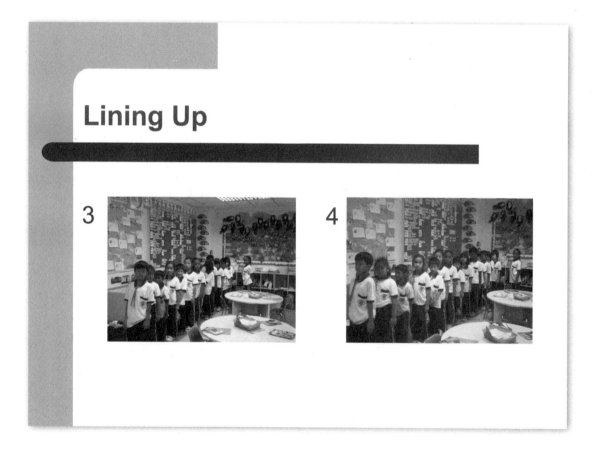

3

4

Being Tidy

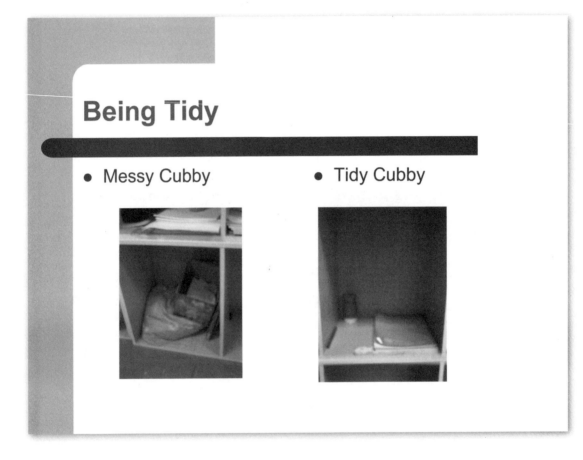

- Messy Cubby

- Tidy Cubby

Cooperating in Class

Doing pair work

Raising hands

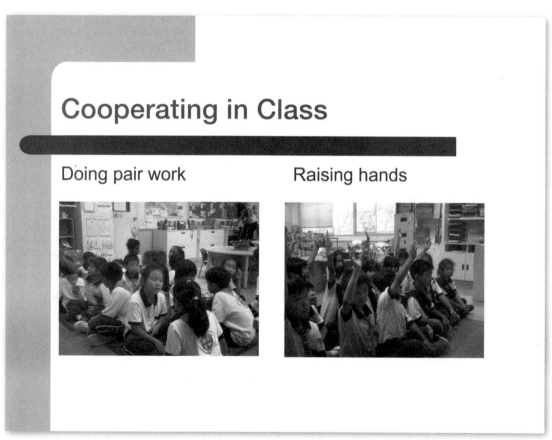

Are you ready?

Not ready   Ready

How to Wear a Tie

The Right Way   The Wrong Way

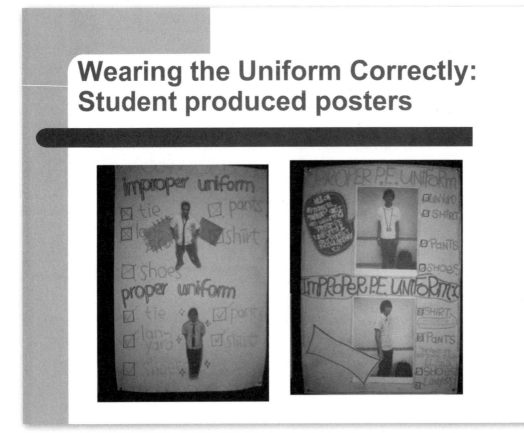

The "Moose" I am ready, looking at the teacher, with empty hands.

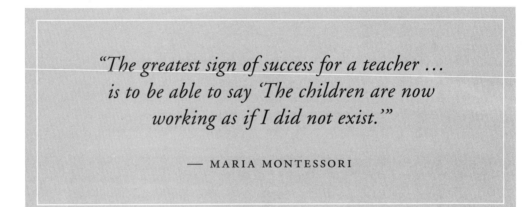

*"The greatest sign of success for a teacher ...
is to be able to say 'The children are now
working as if I did not exist.'"*

— MARIA MONTESSORI

BIBLIOGRAPHY

Avgerinou, M., & Ericson, J. (1997). "A Review of the Concept of Visual Literacy." *British Journal of Educational Technology*, 28(4), 280–291.

Bryan, L. & Gast, D. (2000). "Teaching on-task and on-schedule behaviors to high functioning children with autism via picture activity schedules." *Journal of Autism and Developmental Disorders*, 30, 553–567.

Garretson, H.B., Fein, D., & Waterhouse, L. (1990). "Sustained attention in children with autism." *Journal of Autism and Developmental Disorders*, 20(1), 101–14.

Hyerle, D. (2000). *A Field Guide to Using Visual Tools*. Alexandria, VA: Association for Supervision and Curriculum Development.

Jensen, E. (1997). *Brain Compatible Strategies*. Del Mar, CA: Turner Point Publishing.

Katsioloudis, P. J. (2007). *Identification of Quality Indicators of Visual-Based Learning Material in Technology Education Programs for Grades 7–12.* (Doctoral dissertation). North Carolina State University, Raleigh, NC.

Marzano, R.J., Pickering, D.J. & Pollack, J.E. (2001). *Classroom Instruction that Works: Research-based Strategies for Increasing Student Achievement.* Alexandria, VA: Association for Supervision and Curriculum Development.

Medina, J. (2008). *Brain Rules*. Seattle, WA: Pear Press.

Mesibov, G., Browder, D., & Kirkland, C. (2002). "Using individualized schedules as a component of positive behavior support for students with developmental disabilities." *Journal of Positive Behavior Interventions*, 25, 58–72.

Smith, R. (2004). *Conscious Classroom Management: Unlocking the Secrets of Great Teaching*. Fairfax, CA: Conscious Teaching publications.

Sylwester, R. (1995). *A Celebration of Neurons*. Alexandria, VA: Association for Supervision and Curriculum Development.

Wolfe, P. (2001). *Brain Matters: Translating Research into Classroom Practice.* Alexandria, VA: Association for Supervision and Curriculum Development.

PRAISE FOR KEYNOTES AND WORKSHOPS

For Rick Smith

"You led your phenomenal keynote address the way educators across the world should be leading their classrooms. You taught the strategies yourself along with allowing us to experience the strategies from the 'student' perspective. Bravo!"

— CARLA S., MIDDLE SCHOOL PRINCIPAL

"Thank you for sharing your enthusiastic, energetic, educational presentation with us. Teachers had practical, fun, and immediately usable ideas with which to begin their classes. Your time and effort helped make my teachers feel special, important and ready to start a great year."

— ROSALIE L, ELEMENTARY PRINCIPAL

"Rick Smith is so dynamic and engaging! He's like a young Harry Wong on steroids."

— KATHY P., MIDDLE SCHOOL ENGLISH

"Wow! You articulate things I haven't even thought of sharing with my beginning teachers. Thanks!"

— GEORGE P., MENTOR TEACHER

"Rick gave me the courage to return to the classroom and do what I love doing."

— NORA W., "UN-RETIRED" 4TH GRADE TEACHER

"Rick is a wonder. I am taking so much back with me to share. This is the best I've heard in many years."

— MARIA V., MENTOR TEACHER

Best school start ever! Amazing. Thank You!"

— KATHY D, H.S. MATH

"Rick has super energy and has so much to share. Please have Rick talk to all the teachers in our district!!! You give inspiration to our profession."

— LAURA T., MENTOR TEACHER

"Everything was powerful, but one thing really stood out. That was to assume the best of my students."

— KIM M, 5TH GRADE

"Best workshop I've been to. 'Real' practical ideas and strategies delivered with humor and professionalism. Validated all emotions of (struggling) teachers. Very positive and motivating. Great analogies and metaphors. Kept my interest all day! Rick is fabulous!"

— SUSAN W., 6TH GRADE

For Grace Dearborn's Workshops

"All I can say is Grace was a hit! Even the most jaded teachers—and trust me on this one, we know jaded—have been stopping me in hallways, sending me e-mails, and telling their administrators that Grace was 'the best presenter' we have ever brought in ... Ahhh, success! Thank you, thank you, thank you."

— PAULA, PD FACILITATOR

"Grace Dearborn has provided THE BEST instructional in-service I've ever attended."

— TONY, ENGLISH/MENTOR TEACHER, 28TH YEAR

"Presenter is phenomenal. Knows kids / knows strategies!"

— MATT, 4TH GRADE, 1ST YEAR

"Grace was an exceptional presenter. Her humor and genuine passion came through in every recommendation she put forth. The tools from this workshop will help my students do better and help me keep my sanity."

— JULIE, 3RD GRADE, 2ND YEAR

"Your enthusiasm is contagious. Thank you for reminding all of us about how wonderful kids can be."

— BARBARA, MENTOR TEACHER, 14TH YEAR

"An exceptional workshop taught by a warm, confident, entertaining, and very wise presenter. Grace is passionate and powerful!"

— MATTHEW, MUSIC, 11TH YEAR

"Awesome presentation! Inspiring! Refreshing! Fun!"

— VERONICA, 1ST GRADE, 11TH YEAR

"The absolute best presentation ever! AWESOME!"

— BOB, SPECIAL ED, 12TH YEAR

"I tend to give up on some kids I've tried 'everything' with— and now I feel rejuvenated and ready to start anew—Cheers!"

— BARBARA, 4/5 COMBO, 11TH YEAR

"I got so much out of this workshop, even things that were modeled but not the focus of the presentation. LOVE YOUR HUMOR!!"

— KAREN, PE, 19TH YEAR

"This has been the BEST training I have attended ever! The ideas were realistic and very practical in the 'real' classroom."

— RAYCHELLE, 5TH GRADE, 10TH YEAR

Bright Ideas

Notes

Bright Ideas

Notes

Bright Ideas

Notes

Bright Ideas

Notes

Bright Ideas

Notes

Bright Ideas

Notes

ABOUT THE AUTHORS

Rick Smith

Rick Smith, M.A., is an award-winning teacher, education consultant and international presenter. He has shared practical teaching strategies with more than 100,000 teachers and teacher-trainers worldwide, experience that includes two years training American Peace Corps Volunteer Teachers in Ghana, West Africa.

He has conducted countless keynotes and workshops on effective classroom management and instructional strategies, which are consistently praised for both their motivational and practical value. His groundbreaking book *Conscious Classroom Management: Unlocking the Secrets of Great Teaching* is a best-seller in the United States and abroad.

For more than 14 years, Rick taught in the classroom in San Rafael, California, with a primary focus on at-risk students; he also was a mentor teacher and mentor coordinator for seven years. In addition, he has taught in the Secondary Credential Program at Dominican College in San Rafael, and the Elementary Credential Program at St. Mary's College in Moraga, both in California.

Rick's Master's thesis, entitled *Mentoring New Teachers: Strategies, Structures, and Successes*, appears in *Teacher Education Quarterly,* Autumn, 1993. His article *"Assume the Best for Student Success"* appears in the ASCD magazine *Classroom Leadership*, October 2002. His chapter "Visuals and Classroom Management" appears in *The Praeger Handbook of Learning and the Brain*, 2006.

Rick's goal is to bring out the best in students and teachers by offering teachers nurturing and practical tools for surfing the challenging waves of the classroom experience.

Grace Dearborn

Grace Dearborn facilitates workshops for Conscious Teaching on classroom management and motivating reluctant learners. She also consults for the Strategic Literacy Initiative, training teachers on meta-cognitive reading interventions for adolescent readers. In addition, Grace works locally in the San Francisco Bay Area as a mentor teacher for new and veteran teachers who struggle with behavior management in their classrooms.

Grace's goal is to help the teachers she works with by addressing "what they do" and "who they are." In this way, her trainings and mentoring are both practical and inspirational, leaving an emotional footprint on the schools and teachers with whom she works.

Before entering consulting, Grace taught at multiple grade levels for over a decade in the San Francisco Bay Area. While teaching, Grace also wrote curricula for elementary and secondary schools. Her most recognized work was a year-long literacy intervention social studies course that was taught to all in-coming ninth graders at an urban, low performing high school in Oakland, California. Her course resulted in a dramatic increase in the students' state test scores, raising the school's API by 70 points over three years.

Besides teaching, writing curricula, and consulting, Grace has also held several other positions at the school and district levels. She has worked as a BTSA (Beginning Teacher Support and Assessment) coordinator, Professional Development Coordinator, Literacy Coach, Curriculum Specialist, and Mentor Teacher. Her skills as a behavior specialist are daily put to their truest test by her two sons Owen and Mason, ages five and seven.

Mary Lambert

Mary Lambert is a mediator for California Law and Mediation, Inc., and has been a seminar leader in the Bay Area for the past 25 years with a program called the Grace Release. In her mediation practice, she specializes in communication facilitation and conflict resolution. She provides strategies and environments for her clients, helping to find the resolutions they need.

She also actively leads workshops, retreats, and meditation courses as a teacher and guide, assisting clients to build connections for both inner and outer success. She designs meditation practices based on an individual's current needs, focusing on "becoming your practice," so that meditation is not just a thing you do, but a matter of who you are.

Currently Mary's programs include the Conscious Living Series, a program designed to promote conscious relationship, communication skills, and conflict resolution, making it simple and easy. She has worked with numerous businesses and thousands of people, including individuals, couples, families, and groups.

Mary was the Muse and a key contributor to Rick's first book, *Conscious Classroom Management,* and is currently writing her own book titled *Conscious Living—Releasing Grace and Ending Conflict.*

Mary can be reached at *www.thegracerelease.com.*